Fire Prevention and Fire Extinction

by James Braidwood

FIRST SUPERINTENDENT OF THE LONDON FIRE-BRIGADE, AND ASSOCIATE OF THE INSTITUTION OF CIVIL ENGINEERS.

INCLUDING

FIRE-PROOF STRUCTURES, FIRE-PROOF SAFES, PUBLIC FIRE BRIGADES, PRIVATE MEANS FOR SUPPRESSING FIRES, FIRE-ENGINES, FIRE ANNIHILATORS, PORTABLE FIRE-ESCAPES, WATER SUPPLY

I0439523

CONTENTS.

MEMOIR.

Supply by Water Companies in London

Supplying Fire Engines from fire-cocks, &c.

EDITOR'S PREFACE.

The appearance at the beginning of last year, in the Annual Report of the Institution of Civil Engineers for 1861 and 1862, of a short memoir of Mr. Braidwood, suggested the publication of a more extended account of the life of the late head of the London Fire Brigade, combined with his opinions upon the subject of his profession.

These opinions are comprised in a work on "Fire Engines, and the Training of Firemen," published in Edinburgh in 1830; two papers upon cognate subjects read before the Institution of Civil Engineers, two similar papers read before the Society of Arts, and in a variety of reports upon public buildings, warehouses, &c. While regretting the great loss that the public has sustained, in being deprived by Mr. Braidwood's sudden death of a complete record of his long and varied London experience, it has been considered advisable to republish the above materials arranged in a systematic form, omitting only such parts as the Author's more matured experience rendered desirable, but confining the whole to his own words.

LONDON,

June, 1866.

AUTHOR'S PREFACE

To his work "On the Construction of Fire-Engines and Apparatus; the Training of Firemen; and the Method of Proceeding in cases of Fire," published in Edinburgh, in 1830.

Not having been able to find any work on Fire-Engines in the English language, I have been led to publish the following remarks, in the hope of inducing others to give further information on the subject.

For the style of the work I make no apology; and as I presume no one will read it except for the purpose of gaining information, my aim will be obtained if I shall have succeeded in imparting it, or in directing the public attention to the advantage which may be derived from the systematic training of Firemen.

MEMOIR

OF

JAMES BRAIDWOOD.

The history of mankind, from the earliest times, has been one of alternate peace and war with fire. The immeasurable value of its obedience, and the fearful consequences of its insubordination, have, in all ages, made its due subjection one of the most important conditions of even human existence itself. As camps and trading stations grew into populous cities, the dangers of fire were both multiplied and aggravated. Its ravages in the ancient capitals of the world are matters of history; and it is established that something like organization was extended to the means then employed for suppressing conflagrations. Even the fire-engine itself, in a practicable, although imperfect form, was described and illustrated by a sectional working drawing, by Hero of Alexandria, in a book written by him more than one hundred years before the Christian era. In its many translations, from the original Greek into Latin and into modern tongues, Hero's book, with its remarkable series of drawings, still occupies a place in the mechanical literature of our own time. But, although the construction of the fire-engine was thus known two thousand years ago, we have no actual evidence of its use until within the last two centuries; and within the whole compass of English history, at least, we know that nothing like discipline and organization, in the modern sense of the terms, were introduced into the management of fire apparatus until a time quite within the recollection of the middle-aged men of our own day. If there be anything apparently improbable in this fact, we need only recollect that many of the grandest triumphs of human genius, with which we are already so familiar, are not yet forty years old. The modern system of English fire brigades belongs wholly to the period of railways, steam navigation, and electric telegraphs, and it owes nearly all to the genius and disciplined heroism of a single individual, James Braidwood, who, but little more than four years ago, fell--as nobly for himself as sadly for others--at his chosen post of duty. What, when he first gave his energies--indeed, his whole heart to it, was but the rough and unskilful employment of the fireman, became under Mr. Braidwood's command and his infusing spirit of order and intelligence, as distinguished from reckless daring, a noble pursuit, almost rising in dignity to a profession, and indeed acknowledged as such by many, and significantly, although indirectly, by Royalty itself.

Until the year 1833, not only the parish engines of the metropolis, numbering, as they did, about three hundred, but the engines also of the Fire Insurance Companies, were comparatively inefficient and often out of order, while they were also under the most diverse, if not irresponsible management. There were no really trained firemen, and those who controlled and worked the engines were oftener in antagonism with each other than acting in concert. The parish engines were in the care of the beadles, and in one case a beadle's widow, Mrs. Smith, for some years commanded one of the city engines. The energies of each band of firemen were commonly reserved for the protection of property only in which their own insurance company or parish was immediately interested. As a rule, whatever water was thrown upon a burning building was dashed against the walls, windows, and roof from the outside only, very little if any really reaching the actual seat of the fire within. As a consequence, fires, which are now quickly "got under," were then left to burn themselves out, the spreading of the fire being prevented either by deluging the contiguous buildings with water, or by pulling them down altogether.

James Braidwood was born in Edinburgh in the year 1800. His father was a well-known upholsterer and builder, who appears to have chosen for his son the profession of a surveyor. To this end he was entered at the High School, then under the rectorship of Mr. (afterwards Professor) Pillans, and here, and subsequently under private masters, the youth received a sound education in the branches most appropriate to his intended pursuit in life. He was for some time engaged in his father's business, and thereby gained an amount of practical knowledge, which was of, perhaps, as much service to him in his subsequent career as a fireman, as it would have been had he adopted the profession originally chosen for him. Young Braidwood was an apt student, a fact, perhaps, sufficiently attested afterwards by his successful authorship, at the age of thirty, of the only English work then extant upon the fire-engine and its proper management. He read much, wrote well, was a good draughtsman, and had a sound knowledge of mechanics. But whether his powers required wider scope than a surveyor's practice could offer, or whether, more than forty years ago, and in Edinburgh, the chances of professional success were very much less than now, James Braidwood soon turned his mind to what became the great work of his life. He was becoming known for activity and a high order of personal courage, and there were those in place and power who saw in him the other elements of character which go to make a successful leader of men. He was soon, and when but twenty-three years of age, made the superintendent of the Edinburgh fire engines, and he almost as soon began to reform their inefficient and vicious system of management. He had held his post but three weeks, however, when the series of fires broke forth which still bear the name of the Great Fire of Edinburgh. Many of the old and lofty houses in the High Street were destroyed, between four and five hundred families were made houseless, ten persons were either killed outright or fatally injured, and for several days nearly the whole of the High Street, if not the larger part of the old town, was threatened with destruction. Never were the consequences of want of organization more conspicuous. There was no real command, for there were none to obey; and while those who might have stopped the flames at the outset, wasted their own energies in random efforts, or, perhaps, fell to quarrelling among themselves, the fearful devastation rolled on. The occasion was sufficient to induce the authorities and insurance companies to listen to and profit by Mr. Braidwood's recommendations. They consented to bear in common the expenses necessary to organize and maintain an efficient brigade. This was soon formed of picked men, who, although daily engaged in their former ordinary occupations, were regularly inspected, trained, and exercised early in one morning of every week. Fires were becoming more and more numerous year by year; but the influence of the improved system was soon felt. The men were taught to improve to the utmost the first few minutes after an alarm was given, and by constant emulation and discipline, a spirit of wonderful readiness was cultivated in them. They were trained to seek out and follow up the source of a fire before it had had time to spread, and to throw the water from the engines directly upon it, instead of wastefully, if not injuriously about. The result was, that while out of forty-eight fires which happened in the first year of the history of the brigade, eleven proved total losses, and twelve "considerable" losses, the number of total losses decreased rapidly, year by year, while the whole number of "calls" was almost as rapidly increasing. Thus in the second year of the brigade there were eighty "calls," of which seven were total, and eighteen considerable losses. In the next three years, with from ninety-four to one hundred and ninety-four "calls" yearly, there was but one total loss in each year, and but from nine to eighteen "considerable" losses.

Mr. Braidwood was meanwhile improving the fire-escapes, and when new engines were added to the force, he procured better workmanship. By his personal influence, also, more than by the mere advantage of official position, Mr. Braidwood secured the constant co-operation of the police in giving the earliest alarms of fire, and in facilitating the labours of the firemen when actually on duty. As has just been shown, the results of method, applied skill, and of a personal devotion cultivated under the high impulse of immediate public observation and approval, were soon manifest. To this vast improvement the Edinburgh Mercury, as representing the opinion of the citizens of the Scottish capital, bore public testimony in its issue of August 14, 1828, when the Fire Brigade of that city had been tested by nearly five years of constant trial, and with conspicuous success. Referring to the excellent organization of the establishment, it was remarked that there were then but few, if any, serious fires in Edinburgh, for when a fire broke out--and the alarms were as frequent as ever--it was speedily checked. Said the writer:--

"Not only is the apparatus constructed on the best possible principles, but the whole system of operations has been changed. The public, however, do not see the same bustle, or hear the same noise as formerly; and hence they seem erroneously to conclude that there is nothing done. The fact is, the spectator sees the preparation for action made, but he sees no more. Where the strength of the men and the supply of water used to be wasted, by being thrown against windows, walls, and roofs, the firemen now seek out the spot where the danger lies, and creeping on hands and feet into a chamber full of flame, or smoke, often at the hazard of suffocation, discover the exact seat of danger; and, by bringing the water in contact with it, obtain immediate mastery over the powerful element with which they have to contend. In this daring and dangerous work men have occasionally fainted from heat, or dropped down from want of respiration, in which cases the next person at hand is always ready to assist his companion, and to release him from his service of danger."

In a fire which happened while Mr. Braidwood was at the head of the

Edinburgh Brigade, he won great admiration by bringing out from the burning building a quantity of gunpowder which was known to be stored there. He would not ask any of his men to undertake this dangerous feat, but, amidst the breathless suspense of thousands of spectators, he coolly searched for and safely carried out, first one, and then a second, cask of this explosive material. Had the fire reached the powder, it was known that the worst consequences of the conflagration would have been immensely increased.

The fame of the Edinburgh Brigade rapidly spread throughout the kingdom, and it gradually became regarded as a model to which all other organizations for the suppression of fires would ultimately be made to conform. As a response to constant inquiries from a distance, Mr. Braidwood, in 1829, forwarded to the Society of Arts, London, a description of his chain-ladder fire-escape. For this invaluable apparatus, which had already effected a considerable saving of life, the Society's Silver Medal was awarded, and, accompanying the award, the Council of the Society extended an invitation to the author to "give a complete account of his mode of drilling firemen, and combining the use of fire-escapes with the ordinary fire-engine service." Responding to this invitation, Mr. Braidwood in the following year published his work "On the Construction of Fire-Engines and Apparatus, the Training of Firemen, and the Method of Proceeding in Cases of Fire." From this work, which may still be regarded as an authority, extensive extracts have been made in the subsequent chapters of the present volume, and it need not, therefore, be further referred to here than to say that it formed a thoroughly original account of an original system, and that its illustrations, which were especially clear, were drawn by the author's own hand. This work attracted much attention from municipal bodies and insurance companies throughout the kingdom, and more than one official deputation visited Edinburgh to learn from Mr. Braidwood himself the details of a system which was already working such important results. In London, especially, three West India warehouses had been burnt in the year 1829, with a loss of 300,000l.; and with the extending use of gas, the increasing frequency of fires, and the conspicuous inefficiency of the parish engines, and the want of unity of action among the insurance companies, it was felt that what had answered so well in Edinburgh would prove still more valuable in the metropolis. The general estimation in which Mr. Braidwood's services were then held may be considered as expressed in the following, among other contemporary reviews of his book:--

"The Edinburgh Fire-engine Establishment is now all but perfect. A unity of system has been accomplished, and a corps of firemen mustered, who, in point of physical vigour and moral intrepidity, are all entitled to be denominated chosen men. At the head of this band stands Mr. Braidwood, an individual who has on several occasions given abundant evidence of promptitude in extremity, and a noble contempt of personal danger, and whose enthusiasm, in what we may call his profession, could not have been more strikingly exemplified than by his illustrating it in the manner we now see before us. It is the only book we are acquainted with that treats of the systematic training of firemen; and from the perspicuity of its details, it must necessarily become the manual of all such institutions, and ought to find a place in every insurance office in the United Kingdom."

It had been from time to time attempted to bring the fire apparatus of the London Insurance Companies under a single management; but it was nearly ten years after the establishment of the Edinburgh Fire Brigade, and only when Mr. Braidwood himself had been invited to come to London, that this was at last effected. As for the parish engines, they were wholly neglected under this arrangement, and, indeed, a great number of them had been already allowed to fall into disuse, as far as could be permitted without incurring the penalties of the Statutes of 1774. On the 1st January, 1833, at the instance of Mr. Ford, of the Sun Fire-office, eight of the insurance companies formed an association of fire-engines and firemen, each company withholding its own distinctive name and badges from the united force. This was known as the London Fire-engine Establishment. It was supported by the companies in common, each in proportion to the premiums received from its business in London, a minimum rate being fixed. Each company contributing to the support of the establishment nominated one member of the committee of management. This association existed for thirty-three years, when on the 1st of January, 1866, the Metropolitan Board of Works took charge of the fire-engines and the general fire establishment of the metropolis. Mr. Braidwood took the command of the London Brigade thus formed at the onset. The Edinburgh Fire-engine Committee, on accepting his resignation, presented him with a gold watch, and a vote of thanks, "for the singularly indefatigable manner in which he had discharged the duties of his important office, not merely by his extraordinary exertions on occasions of emergency, but for the care and attention he had bestowed on the training of the firemen, whereby the establishment had been brought to its present high state of efficiency." He had previously received from the men under him a handsome silver cup, bearing the following inscription:--"Presented to Mr. James Braidwood, by the City of Edinburgh Firemen, as a token of their admiration of him as their leader, and of deep respect for him as a gentleman."

As in Edinburgh, the London Fire Brigade under Mr. Braidwood's superintendence became a new force, and in every respect a remarkable organization. Where the inefficiency of the old firemen could not at once be made to yield to discipline, they were pensioned off; and within a short time a select band of active, hardy, and thoroughly trained men was formed. In 1834, the second year of Mr. Braidwood's superintendence, the Houses of Parliament were burnt; and a most destructive fire occurred also at Mile-end. The first-named fire created general consternation, and there are many persons who can still recollect that also at Mile-end. These great fires stimulated Mr. Braidwood to increased exertions, and the result was soon visible in the lessened proportion of totally destroyed premises to the whole number of fires. The brigade had, of course, no power of prevention, and alarms of fire were becoming more numerous than ever. The use of friction matches and of gas was increasing enormously; manufactures, and the steam-engines and machinery for conducting them, were being rapidly multiplied; and with the vast progress making in the production of cotton goods, the use of cotton curtains and bed-furniture was becoming common in dwellings forming a large proportion of the metropolis, but in which, not long before, such articles were either regarded as luxuries or were altogether unknown. The total number of fires attended by the brigade in the year 1833, exclusive of chimneys on fire, was 458, while in 1851 the number had risen to 928; and although London had been growing all this time, it had not doubled in size to correspond with the increased number of fires. But while the total yearly number of fires, since the formation of the brigade, has shown a large and hardly interrupted increase, the number of cases of total destruction has almost as steadily diminished. Thus, "totally destroyed" was reported of 31 fires in the year 1833, whereas in 1839 there were but 17 cases, and the average for twenty-one years, from 1833 to 1853 inclusive, was but 25-1/2 yearly, while at the present time, with all the vast growth of London, the average, under the continuance of Mr. Braidwood's system, is hardly if at all greater.

Mr. Braidwood from the first exhibited excellent judgment in his choice of men to serve under him. He chose sailors, as a rule, as being accustomed to obedience, and to irregular and prolonged duty, while also they were especially hardy and active; and where there was especial danger which must be met, he was always ready to lead, and his men had soon learned to confide in his quick and sound judgment in emergency, knowing that he would never permit them to incur needless risk. His own iron constitution, and his habits of constant vigilance, served as a high standard and incentive to those about him; and thus it was, by selection, discipline, and example, resting upon a foundation of even paternal kindness, that the men of the London Fire Brigade became conspicuous for their courage, energy, hardihood, and unalterable devotion to duty. The brigade, too, was most popular with the public, and could always count upon any necessary assistance in their labours. The system of rewards given to whoever was the first to bring a call of fire, the liberal gratuity to the policeman who first reached the burning premises, there preventing undue confusion, and by keeping the street-door closed, shutting off a strong draught of air from the flames, and the handsome pay to the ready throng of strong-armed men who worked the engines, secured every co-operation from the public, beyond that naturally springing from a general admiration of so brave and well-trained a body of men.

Mr. Braidwood's residence was at the principal station of the Fire-engine Establishment in Watling-street. To this station came all alarms of fire. He attended in person all calls from leading thoroughfares, public buildings, or localities where a serious conflagration might be expected. In the night a call was announced to him through a speaking-tube reaching to his bedside. The gas in his room was always burning, and he would quickly decide, from the known locality of the fire, and from the report given, whether he need go himself. In any case, his men were awake and quickly away. Rapidity in dressing, and in horseing and mounting the engines, was but a detail of daily drill. The moment the scene of action was reached, nothing was allowed to stand in the way of access to the actual seat of the fire, and nothing either in securing a supply of water. The inmates of the premises, if any, were quickly got out, and wherever an unhappy creature was cut off by the flames, there were always one or more firemen ready, if necessary, to brave an apparently certain death in a heroic attempt at rescue--an attempt, indeed, which but seldom failed. It is but just to say here that the firemen were always nobly seconded, if not indeed anticipated, in these attempts by the officers and men of the Royal Society for the Protection of Life from Fire--a body which has long rendered priceless services to humanity under most appalling circumstances. The men of the Fire Brigade were taught to prevent, as much as possible, the access of air to the burning materials. What the open door of the ash pit is to the furnace of a steam-boiler the open street door is to the house on fire. In both cases the door gives vital air to the flames. The men of the Brigade were trained to pursue a fire, not yet under full headway, up-stairs and down, in at windows and out through the roof, anywhere, so it could be reached directly by the water from the engines. They were made to regard it as worse than a waste to throw even a gallon of water upon a dead wall or upon a surface of slate or plaster, so long as by any means the branch pipe could be got to bear upon the seat of the fire itself. The statistics of the operations of the London Fire-engine Establishment from 1833 to the present time, show with what success the system originated and so admirably carried out by Mr Braidwood has been pursued. Of the whole number of fires not one in fifty now proceeds to the extent of total destruction of the premises.

Previous to the organization of the Fire-engine Establishment there were no official annual reports of the fires in the metropolis. No one person by himself was indeed in a position to know all of the fires that happened, any more than, but for Lloyds', could we know of all the wrecks which take place around and upon our coasts. It was impossible, under such a state of things, that either the value of insurance to the insured or its risk to the insurer could be rightly known. The general public could only know that, like fevers and certain other classes of disease, fires were always breaking out, but no one could know, even approximately, how great or how little was the real general risk. When, however, a fire establishment was formed, the engines were called to all fires, whether of insured or uninsured property. It was not now difficult to tabulate the number and localities of fires; but Mr. Braidwood went further, and extended his yearly tables to include the various causes of fires, and the classification of the premises, whether residences, shops, warehouses, manufactories, &c., where they occurred, the subdivision of these classes being extended to every variety of occupation and business. Even the hours at which the various fires broke out were carefully tabulated, and thus the particulars of London fires soon became an important branch of statistics, from which the operations of insurance have derived increased certainty, with greater economy to the insured.

Although regarding the training and discipline of firemen as of the first importance in the organization of a fire brigade, Mr. Braidwood gave a large share of attention to the improvement of fire-engines and their kindred appliances. While in Edinburgh, where the steepness of many of the streets, and the roughness of the pavements in the older parts of the town prevented the rapid and easy movement of heavy engines, he recommended and adopted a lighter description, but in London he recognised the necessity for greater power. Mr. Tilley, then a fire-engine maker in the Blackfriars'-road, ably seconded his efforts, and at length the distinctive type known as the London Fire Brigade Engine was produced, and which, weighing about eighteen cwt. when ready for service, would throw eighty-eight gallons of water per minute, and, in short trials, as much as 120 gallons in the same time. This engine was mounted upon springs, and in strength and ease of working presented a marked improvement upon those which had preceded it. Its ordinary working complement of men was twenty-eight, and larger engines, upon the same general design, have since been made, to be worked by from forty-five to sixty men. The steam fire-engine has already, to a certain extent, superseded the brigade engine, but the latter is still likely, for some time at least, to be preferred for a large class of fires, both in London and in the provinces.

Mr. Braidwood at an early date adopted the ordinary military scaling ladders to the purposes of his brigade, two being placed on each engine, and at his recommendation ladders were also placed on a two-wheeled carriage as a convenient fire-escape. He also induced the Admiralty, in 1841, to adopt hose-reels in the various dockyards, these implements having been previously in successful use in New York. In 1848 he was induced, in consequence of the large number of small fires to which his engines were called out, to adopt a small hand-pump as an auxiliary to the fire-engine. This could be rapidly brought to bear, and although worked by but one man, the value of a small quantity of water thrown directly upon the seat of a small fire was found to be greater than that of perhaps twenty times as much when thrown about in the ordinary manner. It was of great importance also in warehouses stored with valuable goods, to throw the least necessary quantity of water upon a fire. These hand-pumps still form an important part of the present apparatus of the brigade, and they have been widely adopted elsewhere.

London, unlike Edinburgh, has a vast water-side property, always exposed to danger from fire. Almost immediately, therefore, after having taken the command of the London Brigade, Mr. Braidwood directed his attention to the construction of improved floating fire-engines, to be moored in the river, where they would be always available for the protection of wharf property. Two were constructed, one being a machine of great power, with pumps made to be worked by 120 men. These machines proved of great value. In 1852, shortly after the memorable fire at Humphrey's warehouses, he persuaded the Fire-engine Committee to allow one of these engines to be altered so as to work by steam, and in 1855 a large self-propelling floating steam fire-engine was made upon a novel construction, and which, having already rendered great service at fires on the river side, still ranks as the most powerful machine in the service of the brigade. With locomotive boilers and large double steam engines, this float can steam nine miles an hour, and when in place at a fire it can throw four streams of water, each from a jet-pipe of 1-1/2 inch in diameter, to a great distance. In the great fire of 1861, this floating engine was worked with but little intermission for upwards of a fortnight. In 1860 Mr. Braidwood obtained the sanction of the Fire-engine Committee for the introduction of a land steam fire-engine, and although he did not live to witness the present remarkable development of these machines, he was enabled to employ the first one in the brigade with much advantage.

We may quote here from a brief but excellent memoir of Mr. Braidwood, which appeared in the annual report of the Institution of Civil Engineers for 1861:

"As early as 1841, the Government began to profit by his experience, the Lords of the Admiralty having in that year consulted him on the subject of floating fire-engines for the various dockyards. These were eventually constructed from his designs and under his superintendence. In the following year he inspected all the dockyards, and reported fully on each, with regard to both floating and land fire-engines, the supply of water, the alterations of buildings to prevent spread of fire, and the proper care required in dangerous trades. From this time, although not holding any appointment, he acted as Government consulting engineer on all questions relating to fire prevention and extinction, and he advised from time to time the precautions to be taken for the protection of the royal palaces and various other public buildings. This position enabled him, not without a great deal of opposition, to induce the Government to adopt in all its departments a uniform size of hose-coupling. This is the one which he introduced in Edinburgh, and known as the London Fire Brigade coupling, is now in almost universal use; its application has been found comparatively of as much utility for fire-brigade purposes, as the adoption of the Whitworth gauges of screw-bolts for mechanical engineering.

"Although so fully occupied, he never refused advice on professional matters to all who sought it. The various dock companies, public institutions, country fire brigades, private firms, &c., benefited largely by his experience. The numerous inquiries from foreign countries and the colonies with regard to the best means of extinguishing fires, also made great inroads on his time. In 1833 he became an Associate of the Institution of Civil Engineers, to which, in 1844, he contributed a valuable paper 'On the means of rendering large supplies of Water available in case of Fire, &c.,' for which he was awarded a Telford Medal; and in 1849 a second paper 'On Fire-Proof Buildings.' In 1856, a paper on 'Fires: the best means of preventing and arresting them; with a few words on Fire-Proof Structures,' was read by him before the Society of Arts.

"He took great interest in the passing of Acts of Parliament for regulating buildings in the metropolis, was consulted by the framers of these Acts, and used his utmost influence to prevent the endangering a whole neighbourhood by the erection of monster warehouses for private profit. He strongly contended for the principle of dividing buildings by party-walls carried through the roof, and restricting these divisions to a moderate cubic content. Writing to Lord Seymour, Commissioner of Woods and Forests, on the 28th June, 1851, he said 'that no preparations for contending with such fires will give anything like the security that judicious arrangements in the size and construction of buildings will do.' The wise provisions introduced through his instrumentality into these Acts of Parliament were continually being evaded, and clusters of warehouses quickly rose which he saw would, if on fire, defy all his means of extinction. In a letter to Sir W. Molesworth, First Commissioner of Public Works, dated 10th February, 1854, on the subject of a proposed warehouse in Tooley-street, he wrote 'The whole building, if once fairly on fire in one floor, will become such a mass of fire that there is now no power in London capable of extinguishing it, or even of restraining its ravages on every side, and on three sides it will be surrounded by property of immense value.' How literally this was realized, and at what cost, was shown by the great warehouse fire in Tooley-street, on the 22nd June, 1861, at which Mr. Braidwood lost his life."

The great fire at Cotton's Wharf; Tooley-street, broke out on Saturday, June 22nd, 1861, and continued to burn for more than a fortnight, consuming Scovell's, and other large warehouses, and, in all, upwards of two millions' worth of property. The fire is believed to have originated in the spontaneous combustion of hemp, of which upwards of 1000 tons were consumed, together with 3000 tons of sugar, 500 tons of saltpetre, nearly 5000 tons of rice, 18,000 bales of cotton, 10,000 casks of tallow, 1100 tons of jute, and an immense quantity of tea, spices, &c., besides many other descriptions of goods. Although discovered in broad daylight, and before the flames had made any considerable headway, the want of a ready supply of water, and the fact that the iron doors in the division walls between the several warehouses had been left open, taken in connexion with the extremely combustible nature of the materials, soon rendered hopeless all chance of saving the buildings and property. Mr. Braidwood was upon the spot very soon after the alarm had been given, and nearly the whole available force of the Fire-engine Establishment was summoned at his command. He appears to have at once foreseen that the fire would be one of no ordinary magnitude, and that the utmost that could be done would be to prevent its extending widely over adjoining property. The floating fire-engines had been got to bear upon the flames, and the men in charge of the branch pipes were, after two hours' work, already suffering greatly from the intense heat, when their chief went to them to give them a word of encouragement. Several minor explosions, as of casks of tallow or of oil, had been heard, but as it was understood that the saltpetre stored at the wharf was in buildings not yet alight, no alarm was then felt as to the walls falling in. At the moment, however, while Mr. Braidwood was discharging this his last act of kindness to his men, a loud report was heard, and the lofty wall behind him toppled and fell, burying him in the ruins. Those of his men who were near him had barely time to escape, and one person at his side, not a fireman, was overwhelmed with him. From the moment when the wall was seen to fall, it was known that whoever was beneath it had been instantly crushed to death. It is needless, and it would, indeed, be out of place, to describe here the further progress of the fire, which had then but fairly begun, and which was still burning more than a fortnight afterwards.

Great as was the general consternation at so terrible a conflagration, it is doubtful if the public were not still more impressed by the dreadful death of Mr. Braidwood, and by a feeling that his loss was a public misfortune. Her Majesty the Queen, with that ready sympathy which she has ever shown for crushed or suffering heroism, commanded the Earl of Stamford to inquire on the spot, on Monday, whether the body had yet been recovered by the firemen, and Her Majesty's sympathies were also conveyed to Mrs. Braidwood. It was not, however, until the following morning, that after almost constant exertions, under the greatest difficulties, the crushed remains were rescued. An inquest was necessary, not merely to ascertain what was already well known, that death had been instantly caused by accident, but to know whether culpable carelessness of any kind had indirectly led to the sorrowful event. None, however, appeared. The remains of the fallen chief were afterwards borne to his late residence in Watling-street. The members of the committee of the London Fire-engine Establishment, formed of representatives from all of the twenty-five insurance companies of London, had already met to express, by a formal resolution, their sincere condolence with Mrs. Braidwood and her family. It was known that the funeral would take place on Saturday, June 29th, and it was widely felt that a general expression of sorrow and respect should be made, in view of the common loss of so valued a public servant, as well as for the noble qualities for which he had been so long and so well known. On the occasion of the funeral this was shown not more by the great length and marked character of the cortege itself than by the general suspension of business in the leading thoroughfares of the city through which it passed, and by the hushed demeanour of the countless multitude who pressed closely upon the procession throughout its entire course. Among the thousands who sadly led the way to the grave were the London Rifle Brigade, about 700 strong (and of which Mr. Braidwood's three sons were members), the Seventh Tower-Hamlets, and other rifle corps, upwards of 1000 constables of the metropolitan police force, besides nearly 400 members of the city police, the superintendents and men of the various water companies, the secretary and conductors and the band of the Royal Society for the Protection of Life from Fire, a large number of private and local fire-brigades, and the members of the London Fire-engine Establishment. The pall-bearers were six of Mr. Braidwood's engineers and foremen, some of whom were at his side when he fell, and who had barely escaped with their own lives. Following the chief mourners were the Duke of Sutherland, the Earl of Caithness, the Rev. Dr. Cumming, and a large number of relatives and friends of the deceased, and the committee of the London Fire-engine establishment. The procession was nearly one mile and a-half in length, and was about three hours in its progress from Watling-street to Abney Park Cemetery, where the solemn service of the dead was conducted by the Rev. Dr. Cumming, of whose congregation the deceased had long been a member. With the exception of the great bell of St. Paul's, which tolls only on the occasion of the death of a member of the royal family or of a lord-mayor in office, the bells of all the churches in the city were booming slowly through the day, and so evident was the general sorrow that it could be truly said that the heart of the nation mourned.

On Thursday, July 4th, a public meeting was held at the Mansion House, when resolutions were passed for the collection of subscriptions towards a memorial to Mr. Braidwood's long and arduous public services. This memorial, it was felt, should take the form of a permanent provision for his family, for the post of Fire Brigade Superintendent had never been a lucrative one. Before, however, the collection of subscriptions had extended beyond a few hundred pounds, it was made known that the insurance companies had promptly settled upon Mrs. Braidwood the full "value"--speaking in an insurable sense--of her husband's life. Mr. Braidwood had for many years supported two maiden sisters, and the public subscription was applied, therefore, to the purchase of small annuities for each of them.

It will be remembered that the London Fire-engine Establishment was from the first controlled only by the insurance companies, upon whom of course, fell the whole cost of its maintenance. Their interest in the suppression of fires, although direct and unmistakeable, was not the same as that of the public. Thus, it would be to the public advantage that no fires should happen, whereas such a result would be fatal to the insurance companies, since no one in that case would insure. Although the protection of the Establishment was in practice extended alike to both insured and uninsured property, the real object for which it was formed and maintained was undoubtedly that of protecting insured property only. It was the interest of the companies to incur as little expense as would, on the whole, fairly effect this purpose, and it was not their interest to effectually protect the whole of the metropolis from fire. Thus it was that, with all the excellence of the organization and discipline of the Fire-engine Establishment, it was greatly inferior in extent to what was requisite for the proper security of the first city in the world. Mr. Braidwood had long felt this truth, but, acting for a private association, he could only go to the extent of the limited resources at his disposal. It was, more than anything else, the great fire at Cotton's Wharf that first directed public attention to the necessary insufficiency of any private establishment for the general suppression of fires, and that has led to the legislation under which the Fire-engine Establishment was, on the 1st of January last, taken over and extended by the Metropolitan Board of Works. London will now, it is hoped, be better protected from fire, because of the increased extent of the means of protection; but it can hardly be expected that the discipline of the brigade will be improved.

Apart from the public value of Mr. Braidwood's career in increasing the common security against a common foe, there was much in his personal, intellectual, and moral qualities worthy of admiration. He was a man of strong and commanding frame, of inexhaustible energy, and of enduring vitality. The constitutions of but few men could have withstood such long continued wear and tear as fell to his. He braved all weathers, all extremes of heat and cold, could sleep or wake at will, and could work on long after others would have given way. He was always at his post, and in no moment of difficulty or danger did his cool judgment or his steady courage forsake him. It was this, together with his considerate bearing, and on occasions of special trial his almost womanly kindness to his men, that inspired them with unlimited confidence in him and in his plans. Beyond this, he was a man of superior mind, with strong comprehensive and generalising faculties. His various published papers, and a correspondence of which but few could know the extent and importance, as well as his ready, clear, and exact manner in stating his views before committees and before those in authority, who so often consulted him, all attest an order of mind which, in a different sphere, would alone have won distinction for its possessor. His profession was one in which it happens that almost every person thinks himself competent to give advice; yet, without any assumption of authority, Mr. Braidwood could make it felt wherever he pleased that he was a master in the art of extinguishing fire. But he was not on this account the less ready to listen to suggestions, and there are numbers who can bear testimony to the patient, honest, and appreciative manner in which he considered the many and diverse propositions submitted to him as the head of the Fire Brigade of the first city in the world. The soundness of his views and opinions is sufficiently attested by the success of his practice--a success which, but for the Government tax upon fire policies, would have long since made fire insurance in London almost the cheapest of all the forms of protection of property from danger. The London Brigade was insignificant in numbers and tame in display when compared with the eight hundred sapeurs pompiers of Paris, with their parade and all their accessories of effect--insignificant and tame, too, after the glittering apparatus, imposing paraphernalia, and deafening clatter of the "Fire Department" of New York; but Mr. Braidwood's chosen men knew how to do their duty, and considering the differences in the mode of building and of heating, and in the extent of lighting in the three great metropoli just named, it is an easy matter, on reference to statistics, to prove that none others have done better.

Above all, Mr. Braidwood was a gentleman of deep Christian feeling; and those who knew him best had never doubted that, had it been his lot to linger long in pain, knowing the end that was to come, his calm but unwavering faith in a better future would have sustained him through all. Brought up from childhood in the faith of the Scotch church, he was a regular attendant upon the ministrations of the Rev. Dr. Cumming. In his own quiet way he did much good in the poorer districts of London, and he took a special interest in the ragged schools of the metropolis. What he was in his own home may be best inferred from the crushing force with which his dreadful yet noble fate fell upon those who were dearest to him. His family had already too much reason to know the dangers which had always attended his career. A step-son had fallen, five years before, in nearly the same manner, and now lies buried in the same grave. Eleven members, in all, of the brigade, had perished in the discharge of their duty during the time Mr. Braidwood had commanded it: a fact which, taken with daily experience, pointed to other victims to follow. Such consolation, then, as a stricken widow and a mourning family could have, next to an abiding faith in the goodness of God, was in the recollection of the virtues and noble qualities of the husband and father, and in the spontaneous sorrow with which a great people testified their sense of his worth and of their common loss.

To show the universal as well as national esteem in which Mr. Braidwood was held, two extracts are here given from the numerous letters of condolence addressed to his bereaved family, from all parts of the world. Mr. G. H. Allen, Secretary to the Boston (America) Fire Department, writes: "It gives me pleasure to unite with the Board in testimony to the extreme kindness of Mr. Braidwood in the conduct of our correspondence, whereby we have been greatly benefited and received extensive information. Allow me also to extend our sympathy to those who have lost one who will ever be remembered as standing at the head of the most valued arm of the Government, and one that you can hardly expect to be replaced, except by years of experience and great natural ability." Mr. T. J. Bown, Superintendent of the Sydney (Australia) Fire Brigade, in a letter dated 22nd August 1861, says, "On receipt of the sad news, our large fire-bell was tolled, the British ensign hoisted half-mast high, and crape attached to the firemen's uniform, as a token of respect for one of the noblest and most self-denying men that ever lived, who spent and lost his life in the service of his fellow-creatures."

A TRUE HERO.

JAMES BRAIDWOOD.--Died, June 22nd, 1861.

By the Author of

"JOHN HALIFAX, GENTLEMAN."

Not at the battle front,-- Writ of in story; Not on the blazing wreck, Steering to glory;

Not while in martyr pangs Soul and flesh sever, Died he--this Hero new--Hero for ever.

No pomp poetic crown'd, No forms enchained him, No friends applauding watched, No foes arraigned him:

Death found him there, without Grandeur or beauty, Only an honest man Doing his duty:

Just a God-fearing man, Simple and lowly, Constant at kirk and hearth, Kindly and holy:

Death found--and touched him with Finger in flying:-- So he rose up complete-- Hero undying.

Now, all mourn for him, Lovingly raise him Up from his life obscure, Chronicle, praise him;

Tell his last act, done midst Peril appalling, And the last word of cheer From his lips falling;

Follow in multitudes To his grave's portal; Leave him there, buried In honour immortal.

So many a Hero walks Daily beside us, Till comes the supreme stroke Sent to divide us.

Then the Lord calls His own,-- Like this man, even, Carried, Elijah-like, Fire-winged, to heaven.

Macmillan's Magazine, Vol. IV., page 294.

FIRE PREVENTION

INCLUDING

FIRE-PROOF STRUCTURES.

To prevent fires it is necessary to consider what are the principal causes of such calamities. These may be classed under several heads:--

1. Inattention in the use of fires and lights.

2. Improper construction of buildings, &c.

3. Furnaces or close fires for heating buildings, or for mechanical purposes.

4. Spontaneous ignition.

5. Incendiarism.

As almost all fires arise from inattention in one shape or another, it is of the utmost importance that every master of a house or other establishment should persevere in rigidly enjoining and enforcing on those under him, the necessity of observing the utmost possible care in preventing such calamities, which, in nineteen cases out of twenty, are the result of remissness or inattention. Indeed, if any one will for a moment consider the fearful risk of life and property, which is often incurred from a very slight inattention, the necessity of vigilance and care will at once be apparent. Immense hazard is frequently incurred for the most trifling indulgences, and much property is annually destroyed, and valuable lives often lost, because a few thoughtless individuals cannot deny themselves the gratification of reading in bed with a candle beside them.

Some years ago, upwards of 100,000l. were lost, through the partner of a large establishment lighting gas with a piece of paper, which he threw away, and thus set fire to the premises, although it was a strict rule in the place that gas should only be lighted with tapers, which were provided for that purpose. In one department of a great public institution, it was, and is still, a rule that only covered lights should be carried about, and for that purpose four lanterns were provided; yet, on inquiry some time back, it was found that only one was entire, the other three being broken--one having lost two sides and the top; still they were all used as covered lights.

The opportunities for inattention to fires and lights are so various, that it is impossible to notice the whole.

One of the prevailing causes of fire is to be traced to persons locking their doors, and leaving their houses to the care of children. I believe one-half of the children whose deaths are occasioned by accident suffer from this cause alone: indeed, almost every week the newspapers contain some melancholy confirmation of what I have here stated. Intoxication is also a disgraceful and frequent cause of fire. The number of persons burned to death in this way is really incredible. It is true that it does not always happen that a fire takes place in the house, in either of the above cases, although the unfortunate beings whose clothes take fire, rarely escape with their lives; but the danger to the neighbourhood is at all times considerable, if persons in a state of inebriety are left in a house alone. When there is reason to apprehend that any member of a family will come home at night in that state, some one should always be appointed to receive him, and on no account to leave him till he is put to bed, and the light extinguished.

I do not mean to say that people must be actually drunk before danger is to be apprehended from them. Indeed, a very slight degree of inebriety is dangerous, as it always tends to blunt the perception, and to make a person careless and indifferent. I may also add, that no inconsiderable number of fires are occasioned by the thoughtless practice of throwing spirits into the fire. The dresses of females taking fire adds very much to the list of lives lost by fire, if it does not exceed all the other causes put together.

Another very general cause of fire is that of approaching with lighted candles too near bed or window curtains; these, being generally quite dry, are, from the way in which they are hung, easily set on fire, and, as the flames ascend rapidly, when once touched, they are in a blaze in a moment.

It is really astonishing to find that, with daily examples before their eyes, people should persist (whether insured or not seems to make little difference) in practices which, there is a hundred chances to one, may involve both themselves and the neighbourhood in one common ruin. Of this sort are the practices of looking under a bed with a lighted candle, and placing a screen full of clothes too near the fire.

Houses not unfrequently take fire from cinders falling between the joints of the outer and inner hearths. When smoke is observed to arise from the floor, the cause should be immediately ascertained, and the inmates ought on no account to retire to rest while there is the slightest smell of fire, or any grounds to suspect danger from that cause.

Occasional fires are caused by a very absurd method of extinguishing at night the fires kept in grates during the day. Instead of arranging the embers in the grate in such a way as to prevent their falling off, and thus allowing the fire to die out in its proper place, they are frequently taken off and laid on the hearth, where, should there be wood-work underneath, it becomes scorched, and the slightest spark falling through a joint in the stones sets it on fire.

A very frequent cause of fire in shops and warehouses arises from the carelessness of the person intrusted to lock them up. It is no uncommon practice with those to whom this duty is intrusted, to light themselves out, or to search for any little article which may have been mislaid, with a lighted paper, and then to throw it carelessly on the floor, imagining they have taken every necessary precaution, merely by setting their foot upon it, forgetting that the current of air occasioned by shutting the door frequently rekindles it, and produces the most serious consequences.

In warehouses and manufactories, fires are not unfrequently caused by the workmen being occasionally kept late at work. By the time their task is finished, the men are so tired and sleepy, that the extinguishing of fires and lights is done in a very careless manner. I recollect an instance of this sort, in which the flames were issuing from three upper windows, and observed by the neighbours, while the workmen engaged at their employment in the lower floors knew nothing of the destruction that was going on above.

A very serious annual loss is also caused by want of due care in handing up or removing the goods in linen-drapers' shop windows when the gas is burning. Flues taking fire often result in mischief and it is believed that many serious fires have arisen from this cause, which can hardly be called accidental, as, if flues are properly constructed, kept moderately clean, and fairly used, they cannot take fire.

From what has been said, it will be seen that care and attention may do a very great deal towards the prevention of fire, and consequent loss of life. It is very easy to make good rules, and keep them for a time, after having been alarmed by some serious loss of property or life, but the difficulty is to maintain constant attention to the subject. The most evident plan for effecting this seems to be, for the masters thoroughly to examine and consider the subject at certain stated periods, not too far apart, and to constantly warn their domestics, workmen, or others, of the danger of the improper use of fires and lights.

One of the greatest preventives of carelessness in the use of fires and lights would be a legal inquiry in every case, as it would not only show the faults that had been committed, and thus warn others, but the idea of being exposed in the newspapers would be another motive for increased care. This plan has been adopted in New York, and the reports of the proceedings of Mr.

Baker, the "Fire Marshal," show that the inquiries there made have led to most useful results. Mr. Payne, the coroner, held inquests on fires in the City of London some years ago, but the authorities would not allow his expenses, and therefore they were given up, although believed to be highly advantageous in explaining accidental and others causes of fire.

The improper construction of buildings more generally assists the spread than is the original cause of fires, although laying hearths on timber, and placing timber too near flues, are constant causes of fire, and it is believed that many melancholy occurrences have arisen from these and similar sources.

One cause of danger from chimneys arises from the communication which they often have with each other in one gable. The divisions or partitions, being very often found in an imperfect state, the fire communicates to the adjoining chimney, and in this way sometimes wraps a whole tenement in flames. I know a division of a principal street in Edinburgh, in which there is scarcely a single chimney-head that is not more or less in this condition; and I have no doubt that this is not an uncommon case. There is also great danger from the ends of joists, safe-lintels, or other pieces of timber, being allowed to protrude into chimneys. In one instance which came under my notice, a flue passing under the recess of a window had on the upper side no other covering than the wood of the floor; of course, when the chimney took fire the floor was immediately in a blaze: but there are many instances of such carelessness. It is a common practice amongst carpenters to drive small pieces of wood into walls for the purpose of fixing their work, not paying the least attention as to whether the points run into the flues or not.

In the repairs and alterations of old buildings, house-carpenters are, if possible, even more careless in this particular, than in the construction of new.

I know of two different buildings which underwent some alterations. In both of these, safe-lintels had been run into flues, and both of them, after the alterations, took fire; the one in consequence of a foul chimney, which set fire to the lintel; and although the other did not take fire from the same cause, the lintel was nevertheless very much scorched, and obliged to be removed.

Great carelessness is frequently exhibited by builders, when erecting at one time two or three houses connected by mutual gables, by not carrying up the gables, or party-walls, so as to divide the roofs. I have seen more than one instance where the adjoining house would have been quite safe, but for this culpable neglect. It is no uncommon thing, too, to find houses divided only by lath and standard partitions, without a single brick in them. When a fire occurs in houses divided in this manner, the vacuities in the middle of the partitions act like so many funnels to conduct the flame, thereby greatly adding to the danger from the fire, and infinitely increasing the difficulty of extinguishing it.

In London the Building Act forbids all such proceedings, but the District Surveyors do not seem to have sufficient power, or be able to pay sufficient attention to such matters, as they are constantly met with at fires. A very flagrant case of laying a hearth on timber was lately exposed by a fire in the City. Due notice was given of the circumstance, but no farther attention was paid to the matter than to make the proprietor construct the floor properly, although the Act gave power to fine for such neglect. The omission is to be regretted, as there could not have been a better case for warning others; it occurred in a very large establishment, and the work was done by one of the first builders in the City. Had this fire taken place in the night and gained some head, it would have been very difficult to have ascertained the cause. As the premises were situated, a serious loss of life might have occurred, the apartment in which the fire originated being the only means of retreat which ten or twelve female servants had from their bedrooms.

The Metropolitan Building Acts, up to about the year 1825, by insisting upon party-walls and other precautions, were invaluable for the prevention of the spread of fires. By them no warehouse was permitted to exceed a certain area. From the year 1842, the area has been exchanged for a specified number of cubic feet. But since 1825, a class of buildings has arisen of which there are now considerable numbers in the City, called Manchester or piece goods warehouses, which somehow have been exempted from the law restricting the extent of warehouses, on the plea that they are not warehouses, because "bulk is broken" in them, although it is thoroughly understood that the legislature intended by the Act to restrict the amassing such a quantity of goods under one roof as would be dangerous to the neighbourhood.

Manchester and piece goods warehouses have for some time past been built in London of unlimited size, sometimes equal to twenty average houses. This is pretty nearly the same as if that number of houses were built without party-walls, only that it is much worse, for the whole mass generally communicates by well holes and open staircases, and thus takes fire with great rapidity, and, from the quantity of fresh air within the building, the fire makes much greater progress before it is discovered. By this means the risk of fire in the City has been greatly increased, not only to such warehouses themselves, but to the surrounding neighbourhood, for it is impossible to say how far fires of such magnitude may extend their ravages under untoward circumstances, there being at present no preventive power in London capable of controlling them. To provide such a power would be a very costly business.

Such buildings are also against the generally received rule, that a man may burn himself and his own property, but he shall not unduly risk the lives and property of his neighbours.

The new Building Act is likely to repress, to a certain extent, this great evil, unless its meaning be subverted by some such subterfuge as destroyed the efficiency of the last one. But what is to be done with those which are already built? It may seem tedious to dwell so much on this subject, but it appears to be a risk which is not generally much thought of, though it is of the most vital importance to the safety of London. It is very desirable that the metropolis should take warning by the experience of Liverpool, without going through the fiery ordeal which the latter city did.

From 1838 to 1843, 776,762l. were lost in Liverpool by fire, almost entirely in the warehouse risks. The consequence was, that the mercantile rates of insurance gradually rose from about 8s. per cent. to 30s., 40s., and, it is said, in some cases, to 45s. per cent. Such premiums could not be paid on wholesale transactions, therefore the Liverpool people themselves obtained an Act of Parliament, 6 and 7 Vic., cap. 109, by which the size and height of warehouses were restricted, party walls were made imperative, and warehouses were not allowed to be erected within thirty-six feet of any other warehouse, unless the whole of the doors and window-shutters were made of wrought iron, with many similar restrictions. This Act applied to warehouses already built as well as to those to be built, and any tenant was at liberty, after notice to his landlord, to alter his warehouse according to the Act, and to stop his rent till the expense was paid. Another Act, 6 and 7 Vic., cap. 75, was also obtained, for bringing water into Liverpool for the purpose of extinguishing fires and watering the streets only. It is supposed that the works directed, or permitted, by these two Acts, cost the people of Liverpool from 200,000l. to 300,000l. Shortly after these alterations had been made, the mercantile premiums again fell to about 8s. per cent.

There is another very common cause of fire, which seems to come under the head of construction--viz., covering up a fireplace when not in use with wood or paper and canvas, &c. The soot falls into the fireplace, either from the flue itself, or from an adjoining one which communicates with it. A neighbouring chimney takes fire; a spark falls down the blocked-up flue, sets fire to the soot in the fireplace, which smoulders till the covering is burned through, and thus sets fire to the premises.

In theatres, that part of the house which includes the stage and scenery should be carefully divided from that where the spectators assemble by a solid wall carried up to, and through the roof. The opening in this wall for the stage should be arched over, and the other communications secured with iron doors, which would be kept shut while the audience was in the house. By this plan, there would be abundance of time for the spectators to retire, before fire could reach that part of the theatre which they occupy.

The danger from furnaces or close fires, whether for heating, cooking, or manufacturing purposes, is very great, and no flue should be permitted to be so used, unless it is prepared for the purpose. The reason is, that in a close fire the whole of the draught must pass through the fire. It thus becomes so heated that, unless the flue is properly built, it is dangerous throughout its whole course. In one instance of a heating furnace, the heat in the flue was found to be 300? at a distance of from forty to fifty feet from the fire. In open fireplaces, the quantity of cold air carried up with the draught keeps the flue at a moderate heat, from the fire upwards, and, unless the flue is allowed to become foul, and take fire, this is the safest possible mode of heating.

Heating by hot air, steam, and hot water are objectionable. First, because there must be a furnace and furnace flue, and the flue used is generally that built for an open fire only; and second, the pipes are carried in every direction, to be as much out of sight as possible. By this means they are constantly liable to produce spontaneous ignition, for there appears to be some chemical action between heated iron and timber, by which fire is generated at a much lower temperature than is necessary to ignite timber under ordinary circumstances. No satisfactory explanation of this fact has yet been given, but there is abundant proof that such is the case. In heating by hot-water pipes, those hermetically sealed are by far the most dangerous, as the strength of the pipes to resist the pressure is the only limit of the heat to which the water, and of course the pipes, may be raised. In some cases a plug of metal which fuses at 400° is put into the pipes, but the heat to which the plug is exposed will depend very much on where it is placed, as, however great may be the heat of the exit pipe, the return pipe is comparatively cool. But even where the pipes are left open, the heat of the water at the furnace is not necessarily 212°? It is almost needless to say that 212° is the heat of boiling water under the pressure of one atmosphere only; but if the pipes are carried sixty or seventy feet high, the water in the furnace must be under the pressure of nearer three atmospheres than one, and therefore the heat will be proportionately increased. Fires from pipes for heating by hot water have been known to take place within twenty-four hours after first heating, and some after ten years of apparent safety.

The New Metropolitan Building Act prescribes rules for the placing steam, hot-air, and hot-water pipes at a certain distance from timber; but as it must be extremely difficult for the District Surveyors to watch such minute proceedings, it becomes every one who is anxious for safety to see that the District Surveyors have due notice of any operation of this kind.

Another cause of fire which may come under this head is the use of pipes for conveying away the products of combustion. Every one is acquainted with the danger of stove pipes, but all are not perhaps aware that pipes for conveying away the heat and effluvia from gas-burners are also very dangerous when placed near timber. It is not an uncommon practice to convey such pipes between the ceiling and the flooring of the floor above. This is highly dangerous. Gas-burners are also dangerous when placed near a ceiling. A remarkable instance of this took place lately, where a gas-burner set fire to a ceiling 28-1/2 inches from it.

Another evil of furnaces is, that the original fireplace is sometimes not large enough to contain the apparatus, and the party wall is cut into. Perhaps it may be necessary to notice at this point the use of gas, as it is becoming so very general. Gas, if carefully laid on, and properly used, is safer than any other light, so far as actually setting fire to anything goes, but the greater heat given out so dries up any combustibles within its reach, that it prepares them for burning, and when a fire does take place, the destruction is much more rapid than in a building lighted by other means. Gas-stoves, also, from the great heat given out, sometimes cause serious accidents; in one instance, a gas-stove set fire to a beam through a two-and-half inch York landing, well bedded in mortar, although the lights were five or six inches above the stone. This is mentioned to show that gas-stoves require quite as much care as common fires.

Spontaneous ignition is believed to be a very fruitful cause of fires; but, unless the fire is discovered almost at the commencement, it is difficult to ascertain positively that this has been the cause. Spontaneous ignition is generally accelerated by natural or artificial heat. For instance, where substances liable to spontaneous ignition are exposed to the heat of the sun, to furnace flues, heated pipes, or are placed over apartments lighted by gas, the process of ignition proceeds much more rapidly than when in a cooler atmosphere. Sawdust in contact with vegetable oil is very likely to take fire. Cotton, cotton waste, hemp, and most other vegetable substances are alike dangerous. In one case oil and sawdust took fire within sixteen hours; in others, the same materials have lain for years, until some external heat has been applied to them. The greater number of the serious fires which have taken place in railroad stations in and near London have commenced in the paint stores. In a very large fire in an oil warehouse, a quantity of oil was spilt the day before and wiped up, the wipings being thrown aside. This was believed to have been the cause of the fire, but direct proof could not be obtained. Dust-bins also very often cause serious accidents. In one instance, 30,000l. to 40,000l. were lost, apparently from hot ashes being thrown into a dust-bin.

These accidents may in a great measure be avoided by constant care and attention to cleanliness, and where paints and oils are necessary, by keeping them in some place outside the principal buildings. Dust-bins should, as much as possible, be placed in the open air, and where that cannot be done, they should be emptied once a day. No collection of rubbish or lumber of any sort should be allowed to be made in any building of value.

Mr. Wyatt Papworth, architect, has published some very interesting notes on spontaneous ignition, giving several well-authenticated instances.

Incendiarism may be divided into three sorts--malicious, fraudulent, and monomaniac. Of the former there has been very little in London for many years. The second, however, is rather prevalent. The insurance offices, which are the victims, protect themselves as well as they can, but an inquest on each fire is the true mode of lessening the evil. This is much more the interest of the public than at first seems to be the case. In several instances where the criminals were brought to punishment by Mr. Payne's inquests, people were asleep in the upper parts of the houses set fire to, and in one case there were as many as twelve or fifteen persons. This, however, is seldom stated in the indictment, as, if it is, the punishment is still death by the law, and it is supposed that a conviction is more easily obtained, by the capital charge being waived. Monomania is a rare cause of incendiarism, but still several well-certified cases have occurred in which no possible motive could be given. In one instance a youth of fifteen set fire to his father's premises seven times within a few hours. In another, a young female on a visit set fire to her friend's furniture, &c., ten or eleven times in the course of one or two days. In neither case could anything like disagreement or harshness be elicited, but the reverse. In other instances, it has been strongly suspected that this disease was the cause of repeated fires, but there was no positive proof. In all these cases, known or suspected, the parties were generally from fourteen to twenty years of age.

FIRE-PROOF STRUCTURES.

What is "Fire-proof Construction?" is a question which has given rise to a great deal of discussion, simply, as it appears to me, because the size of the buildings, and the quantity and description of the contents, have not always been taken into account. That which may be perfectly fireproof in a dwelling house, may be the weakest in a large warehouse. Suppose an average-sized dwelling-house 20 ?40 ?50 = 40,000 cubic feet, built with brick partitions, stone or slate stairs, wrought-iron joists filled in with concrete, and the whole well plastered. Such a house will be practically fire-proof, because there is no probability that the furniture and flooring in any one room, would make fire enough to communicate to another. But suppose a warehouse equal to twenty such houses, with floors completely open, supported by cast-iron pillars, and each floor communicating with the others by open staircases and wells; suppose, further, that it is half filled with combustible goods, and perhaps the walls and ceilings lined with timber. Now, if a fire takes place below, the moment it bursts through the upper windows or skylights, the whole place becomes an immense blast furnace; the iron is melted, and in a comparatively short time the building is in ruins, and, it may be, the half of the neighbourhood destroyed. The real fire-proof construction for such buildings is groined brick arches, supported on brick pillars only. This mode of building, however, involves so much expense, and occupies so much space, that it cannot be used with advantage. The next best plan is to build the warehouses in compartments of moderate size, divided by party-walls and double wrought-iron doors, so that if one of these compartments takes fire, there may be a reasonable prospect of confining the fire to that compartment only. Again, cast iron gives way from so many different causes, that it is impossible to calculate when it will give way. The castings may have flaws in them; or they may be too weak for the weight they have to support, being sometimes within 10 per cent., or less, of the breaking weight. The expansion of the girders may thrust out the side walls. For instance, in a warehouse 120 feet ×75 feet ×80 feet, there are three continuous rows of girders on each floor, with butt joints; the expansion in this case may be twelve inches. The tie rods to take the strain of the flat arches must expand and become useless, and the whole of the lateral strain be thrown on the girders and side walls, perhaps weak enough already. Again, throwing cold water on the heated iron may cause an immediate fracture. For these and similar reasons, the firemen are not permitted to go into warehouses supported by iron, when once fairly on fire.

Cast and wrought-iron have been frequently fused at fires in large buildings such as warehouses, sugar houses, &c., but according to Mr. Fairbairn's experiments on cast iron in a heated state, it is not necessary that the fusing point should be attained to cause it to give way.[A] He also states, that the loss of strength in cold-blast cast iron, in a variation of temperature from 26° to 190° = 164° Fahr., is 10 per cent., and in hot-blast at a variation of from 21° to 190° = 169° Fahr., is 15 per cent.; now if the loss of strength advances in anything like this ratio, the iron will be totally useless as a support, long before the fusing point is attained.

Much confidence has been placed in wrought-iron tie or tension rods, to take the lateral strain of the arches, and also in trusses to support the beams; but it must be evident that the expansion of the iron from the heat, would render them useless, and under a high temperature, it would be so great as to unsettle the brickwork, and accelerate its fall, on any part of the iron-work giving way: again, the application of cold water to the heated iron, in an endeavour to extinguish the fire, is almost certain to cause one or more fractures. The brick-arching is also very liable to fall, especially if only four and a half inches thick, independently of the weight which may be placed upon it, for it is not uncommon after a fire in a large building, to find the mortar almost completely pulverized to the depth of three inches, or four inches, from the face of the wall. When a fire occurred under one of the arches of the Blackwall Railway, on the 15th July, 1843, a portion of the lower ring fell down, and also a few bricks from the next ring.

Another very serious objection to buildings of this description, is that, unless scientifically constructed, they are very unlikely to be safe, even for the common purposes intended, independent of the risk of fire. In the Report of Sir Henry De la B 阢 he and Mr. Thomas Cubitt on the fall of the mill at Oldham, in October, 1844,[B] it is stated that the strength of the iron-beams was within ten per cent. of the breaking weight. Now according to Mr. Fairbairn's experiments on heated iron, already referred to, an increase of temperature of only 170?would have destroyed the whole building. It is quite clear, therefore, that so long as mill-owners and others continue to construct such buildings without proper advice, they must be liable to these accidents. In timber-floors there can be no such risk, as the strains are all direct, and any journeyman carpenter, by following good examples, can ascertain the size required; and even if he makes a mistake, the evil is comparatively trivial, as the timber will give notice before yielding, and may be propped up for the time, until it can be properly secured. In the case of fire-proof buildings, an ignorant person may make many mistakes without being aware that he has done so, and the slightest failure is probably fatal to every one within the walls. This also increases the difficulty and danger of extinguishing fires in a large building, as the only method of doing so is for the firemen to enter it with their branches, and in case of the floors falling, there is no chance of escape. On the other hand, timber-floors have repeatedly fallen while the firemen were inside the building, and they have made their escape uninjured.

In a pamphlet published by Mr. S. Holme, of Liverpool, in 1844,[C] and which contains a report from Mr. Fairbairn on fire-proof buildings, it is stated, that many people, especially in the manufacturing districts, are their own architects; that the warehouses in Liverpool may be loaded to one ton per yard of flooring; and that unless great care and knowledge are used in the construction of fire-proof buildings, they are of all others the most dangerous.[D]

The following are the principles on which Mr. Fairbairn proposes to build fire-proof warehouses:--

The whole of the building to be composed of non-combustible materials, such as iron, stone, or bricks.

In order to prevent fire, whether arising from accident or spontaneous combustion, every opening, or crevice, communicating with the external atmosphere to be closed.

An isolated staircase, of stone, or iron, well protected on every side by brick, or stone walls, to be attached to every story, and be furnished with a line of water-pipes, communicating with the mains in the street, and ascending to the top of the building.

In a range of stores, the different warehouses to be divided by strong partition-walls, in no case less than eighteen inches thick, and no more openings to be made than are absolutely necessary for the admission of goods and light.

That the iron columns, beams, and brick arches be of strength sufficient, not only to support a continuous dead pressure, but to resist the force of impact to which they are subject by the falling of heavy goods upon the floors.

That in order to prevent accident from the columns being melted by intense heat in the event of fire in any of the rooms, a current of cold air should be introduced into the hollow of the columns, from an arched tunnel under the floors.

There is no doubt that if the second principle could be carried out, namely, the total exclusion of air, the fire would go out of itself; but it seems, to say the least of it, very doubtful indeed if this can be accomplished, and if it could, the carelessness of a porter leaving open one of the doors or windows, would make the whole useless. The fifth principle shows that Mr. Fairbairn has omitted to allow for the loss of strength the iron may sustain from the increase of temperature. The last principle would not be likely to answer its purpose, even if it was possible to keep these tunnels and hollow columns clear for a number of years, which is scarcely to be expected. A piece of cast-iron pipe, one-and-a-half inch in diameter, was heated for four minutes in a common forge, both ends being carefully kept open to the atmosphere, when, on one end being fixed in a vice, and the other pulled aside by the hand, it gave way.

One of the principal objections to the kind of fire-proof buildings above described, is, that absolute perfection in their construction is indispensable to their safety; whereas buildings of a more common description are comparatively safe, although there may be some errors or omissions in their construction. Indeed, Mr. Fairbairn states in the same Report, that "it is true that negligence of construction on the one hand, and want of care in management on the other, might entail risk and loss to an enormous extent."

The following is a very clear proof of the inability of cast iron to resist the effects of fire:--

"A chapel in Liverpool-road, Islington, seventy feet in length and fifty-two feet in breadth, took fire in the cellar, on the 2nd October, 1848, and was completely burned down. After the fire, it was ascertained that of thirteen cast-iron pillars used to support the galleries, only two remained perfect; the greater part of the others were broken into small pieces, the metal appearing to have lost all power of cohesion, and some parts were melted. It should be observed, that these pillars were of ample strength to support the galleries when filled by the congregation, but when the fire reached them, they crumbled under the weight of the timber only, lightened as it must have been by the progress of the fire."

In this case it mattered little whether the pillars stood or fell, but it would be very different with some of the large wholesale warehouses in the City, where numbers of young men sleep in the upper floors; in several of those warehouses the cast-iron pillars are much less in proportion to the weight to be carried than those referred to, and would be completely in the draught of a fire. If a fire should unfortunately take place under such circumstances, the loss of human life might be very great, as the chance of fifty, eighty, or one hundred people escaping in the confusion of a sudden night alarm, by one or two ladders, to the roof, could scarcely be calculated on, and the time such escape must necessarily occupy, independent of all chance of accidents, would be considerable.

For the reasons here stated, I submit that large buildings, containing considerable quantities of combustible goods, with floors of brick-arches, supported by cast-iron beams and columns, are not, practically speaking, fire-proof; and that the only construction which would render large buildings fire-proof; where considerable quantities of combustible goods are deposited, would be groined brick-arches, supported by pillars of the same material, laid in proper cement. I am fully convinced, from a lengthened experience, that the intensity of a fire,--the risk of its ravages extending to adjoining premises, and also the difficulty of extinguishing it, depend, cæteris paribus, on the cubic contents of the building which takes fire, and it appears to me that the amount of loss would be very much reduced, if, instead of building immense warehouses, which give the fire a fortified position, warehouses were made of a moderate size, with access on two sides at least, completely separated from each other by party-walls, and protected by iron-doors and window-shutters. In the latter case, the probability is, that not more than one warehouse would be lost at a time, and perhaps that one would be only partially injured.

It is sincerely to be hoped that the clause in the last Metropolitan Building Act, restricting the size of warehouses, may be more successful than its predecessor, for it is not only property that is at stake, but human life. In many of these "Manchester warehouses," there are fifty or one hundred and upwards of warehousemen and servants sleeping in the upper floors, whose escape, in case of fire, would be very doubtful, to say the least of it.[E]

Covering timber with sheet-iron is very often resorted to as a protection against fire. I have never found it succeed; but Dr. Faraday, Professor Brande,

Dr. D. B. Reid, and Mr. W. Tite, M.P., are of opinion that it may be useful against a sudden burst of flame, but that it is worse than useless against a continued heat.

In wadding manufactories the drying-rooms were frequently lined with iron-plates, and when a fire arose there, the part covered with iron was generally found more damaged than the rest; the heat got through the sheet-iron, and burnt the materials behind it, and there was no means of touching them with water until the iron was torn down; sheet iron should not, therefore, be used for protecting wood.

Even cast iron, one inch thick, laid on tiles and cement three inches thick, has allowed fire to pass through both, to the boarding and joisting below, merely from the fire in an open fire-place being taken off and laid on the hearth. This arises from iron being so good a conductor that, when heat is applied to it, it becomes in a very short time nearly as hot on the one side as the other. If the smoke escapes up a chimney, or in any other way, there may be a serious amount of fire before it is noticed.

In a fire at the Bank of England, the hearth on which the stove was placed was cast iron an inch thick, with two-and-a-half inches of concrete underneath it; but the timber below that was fired.

With regard to the subject of fire-proof dwelling-houses of average size, I consider that such houses when built of brick or stone, with party-walls carried through the roof; the partitions of brick, the stairs of slate or stone, the joists of wrought iron filled in with concrete, and the whole well plastered, are practically fire-proof because, as stated at the opening of this chapter, there is no probability that the furniture and flooring in any one room would make fire enough to communicate to another. The safest manner of heating such houses is with open fire-places, the hearths not being laid upon timber. Stone staircases, when much heated, will fracture from cold water coming suddenly in contact with them; but in a dwelling-house built as described above, there is very little chance of such a circumstance endangering human life, even with wooden steps carried upon brick walls, and rendered incombustible by a ceiling of an inch and a quarter of good hair mortar and well pugged, all the purposes of safety to human life would be attained.

There is a particular description of floor, which, although not altogether fire-proof, is certainly (at least so far as I can judge), almost practically so for dwelling-houses. It is composed simply of plank two and a-half or three inches thick, so closely joined, and so nicely fitted to the walls, as to be completely air-tight. Its thickness and its property of being air-tight, will be easily observed to be its only causes of safety. Although the apartment be on fire, yet the time required to burn through the floor above or below, will be so great, that the property may be removed from the other floors, or, more probably, if the means of extinguishing fire be at hand, it may be subdued before it can spread to any other apartment. The doors must of course be made in proportion, and the partitions of brick or stone.

Before closing the subject of fire-proof structures, I will add a few words upon fire-proof safes. These are all constructed with double casings of wrought iron, the interstices being in some filled with non-combustible substances, such as pumice stone and Stourbridge clay, and in others with metal tubes, that melt at a low temperature, and allow a liquid contained in them to escape, and form steam round the box, with the intention of preventing the heat from injuring the contents. Such safes I have never found destroyed; and in some cases, after large fires, the whole of the contents have been found uninjured, while the papers in common safes, merely made strong enough to prevent their being broken into, were generally found consumed.

FOOTNOTES:

[Footnote A: Vide Seventh Report of the British Association, 1837, vol. vi. page 409.]

[Footnote B: Vide Report on the Fall of the Cotton Mill, at Oldham, and part of the Prison at Northleach, page 4. Folio. London: Clowes and Sons, 1845.]

[Footnote C: Vide Report of W. Fairbairn, Esq., on the Construction of Fire-proof Buildings. With introductory Remarks by Samuel Holme, page 11, et seq. Tract, 8vo. Liverpool: T. Baines, 1844.]

[Footnote D: The Author has been informed by Mr. Farey, M. Inst. C.E., that a fire took place, in 1827, in a mill belonging to Mr. Marshall, of Leeds, the whole of which, with the exception of the roof, was fire-proof. The upper floor was filled with flax, which took fire; the roof fell in, and the heat so affected the iron beams of the floor, as to cause them to give way.]

[Footnote E: In the year 1858, when reporting to the Insurance Offices upon the Warehouses in the Metropolitan Docks, Mr. Braidwood made the following suggestions which are applicable to all large buildings. That all the party-walls where the roofs do not rise above the wall, should be 3 feet 6 inches above such roof. That all the party-walls in the valleys of the roofs should be raised to the level of the highest ridge on either side, all openings in such walls being closed by wrought-iron doors on each side of the walls, at least a quarter of an inch thick in the panels, and such openings not to exceed 42 superficial feet in the clear. That all windows which look upon other windows, or loop-hole doors in other warehouses or compartments, within 100 feet, should be bricked up, or have wrought-iron shutters at least 3/16th of an inch thick in the panels.

That all loop-hole doors similarly situated should be made entirely of wrought iron, frames included, or bricked up. That all shafts for lifts or other purposes, should be of brick, with wrought-iron doors where necessary to receive or deliver goods, and that all openings whatever for machinery should be included in such shaft. That every hatchway or opening in the floors for "shooting" goods from floor to floor should have a strong flap hinged on to the floor, to be closed when not in use, especially at night.

That there should be direct access to every room, of every compartment, of every warehouse, from a fire-proof staircase, by iron doors, and that all such staircases should enter from the open air, as well as from under any warehouse on the quay; in the latter case the doors must be of iron only.

All the windows in the entresol and ground floors to be bricked up, or have iron shutters, and the doors and frames to be of iron.

Wherever the warehouses face each other within 100 feet, the front parapet walls to be carried up to the level of the ridge of the roof.

When it is stated in this report that the windows or loop-hole doors should be bricked up, it is not meant to exclude the use of thick glass, three or four pieces being built into each door or window space, not exceeding 6 inches in diameter or square, in the clear, and set in the mortar or cement at least 3/4 of an inch all round, the glass to be not less than 1-1/2 inches thick, flat on both sides, and so placed that no goods can be stored within 18 inches of the inner surface.

There should be a tank on the top of each staircase, with a tap from it on each landing, with six fire buckets hung near it, and three small hand pumps in every staircase; the officers and workpeople seeing these every day would be certain to run to them in case of fire, and by having a constant supply of water on every floor small accidents might be extinguished at once, and the iron doors and roofs kept cool in case of one room taking fire.]

FIRE EXTINCTION, INCLUDING FIRE BRIGADES, FIRE ENGINES, AND WATER SUPPLY.

Before entering upon the subject of Public Fire Brigades, I will call attention to the course to be pursued by inmates of the house on fire, and their neighbours.

When all available means of fire prevention have been adopted, the next thing to be considered is a supply of water. In the country, or where there are no water-pipes or engines, this ought to be particularly attended to, and a hand-pump should be provided. Where no water is kept solely for the purpose of extinguishing fire, such vessels as can be spared should be regularly filled every night, and placed in such situations as may be most convenient in case of danger; and no master of a family ought to retire to rest, without being satisfied that this has been attended to. If it had no other advantage than merely that of directing the inmates of a house to the possibility of such an occurrence as fire, it would be worth much more than the trouble such an arrangement would cost; but, in addition to that, a supply of water would be at hand, in most cases more than sufficient to extinguish the fire immediately on its being discovered, and before it had become either alarming or dangerous. But when no such precaution has been adopted, when even the bare possibility of fire has not been considered, when no attention has even been paid to the subject, and no provision made for it; the inhabitants are generally so alarmed and confused, that the danger is probably over, by their property being burned to the ground, before they can sufficiently recollect themselves to lend any effective assistance.

In most cases of fire, the people in whose premises it occurs are thrown into what may be called a state of temporary derangement, and seem to be actuated only by a desire of muscular movement, no matter to what purpose their exertions are directed. Persons may often be seen toiling like galley-slaves, at operations which a moment's reflection would show were utterly useless. I have seen tables, chairs, and every article of furniture that would pass through a window, three or four stories high, dashed into the street, even when the fire had hardly touched the tenement. On one occasion I saw crockery-ware thrown from a window on the third floor.[F]

Most of these extravagances take place on the first alarm. When the engines have got fairly into play, people begin to recollect themselves, and it is at this time that most of those "who go to see a fire" arrive. By the exertions of the police there is then generally a considerable degree of order restored, and the most interesting part of the scene is over.

What remains, however, may, from its novelty or grandeur, if the fire is extensive, be still worth looking at for a little, but much of the excitement is banished with the confusion; and if the fire and firemen seem to be well matched, the chief interest which is excited in the spectators is to ascertain which of the parties is likely to be victorious. Few people, comparatively, have thus an opportunity of witnessing the terror and distraction occasioned by the first alarm of fire, and this may probably account for the apathy and indifference with which people who have not seen this regard it.

When a fire actually takes place, every one should endeavour to be as cool and collected as possible; screams, cries, and other exhibitions of terror, while utterly useless in themselves, have generally the effect of alarming those whose services might otherwise be of the utmost advantage, and of rendering them unfit for useful exertion. It is unhappily, too, at the commencement of fires, that this tendency to confusion and terror is the strongest, when a bucket of water, properly applied, is generally of more value than a hundred will be half an hour afterwards. It is the feeling of total surprise, on the breaking out of a fire, which thus unhinges the faculties of many individuals. They have never made the case their own, nay, one would almost imagine they had scarcely thought such an occurrence possible, till, coming on them almost like a thunderbolt, they are lost in perplexity and terror. The only preventive against this is to think the matter over frequently and carefully before it occurs.

The moment it is ascertained that fire has actually taken place, notice should be sent to the nearest station where there is a fire-engine. No matter whether the inmates are likely to be able to extinguish the fire themselves-- this should never be trusted to if more efficient help can be had.

It is much better that an engine should be turned out twenty times when it is not wanted, than be once too late. This may cause a trifling expense; but even that expense is not altogether lost, as it teaches the firemen steadiness and coolness.

The person in the house best qualified for such duty should endeavour to ascertain, with as much precision as possible, the extent and position of the fire, while the others collect as much water as they can. If the fire be in an upper floor, the inmates should be got out immediately, although the lower part of the house may generally be entered with safety for some time. If in the lower part of the house, after the inmates have been removed, great care should be observed in going into any of the upper floors, as the flames very often reach the stair before being observed by those above. The upper floors are, besides, generally filled with smoke, and, in that case, there is great danger of suffocation to those who may enter.

This, indeed, is the principal danger attending fires, and should be particularly guarded against, as a person, when being suffocated, is unable to call for assistance. In a case of this kind the fire took place in the third floor from the street, and all the inmates immediately left the premises except one old woman. In about fifteen minutes after the arrival of the engines, the firemen made their way upstairs, and the poor woman was found dead beside a basket partly filled with clothes, which it was supposed she had been packing up for removal; had she made any noise, or even broke a pane of glass, she would, in all probability, have been saved; as the fire never touched the floor in which she was found, she must have died entirely from suffocation, which a little fresh air would have prevented. Had the slightest suspicion existed that any one was in the upper floors, they would have been entered by the windows or the roof; but as the fire took place in daylight, and none of the neighbours spoke of any one being in the house, it was thought unnecessary to damage the property, or risk the lives of the firemen, without some adequate cause. This, however, shows how little dependence can be placed on information received from the inmates of the premises on fire. Some of the people who lived on the same floor with this poor woman, and who had seen her immediately before they left the house, never mentioned her. I do not suppose that this negligence arose from apathy, or any feeling of that sort; but the people were in such a state of utter confusion, that they were unable to think of anything. But to return.

On the first discovery of a fire, it is of the utmost consequence to shut, and keep shut, all doors, windows, or other openings. It may often be observed, after a house has been on fire, that one floor is comparatively untouched, while those above and below are nearly burned out. This arises from the door on that particular floor having been shut, and the draught directed elsewhere. If the person who has examined the fire finds a risk of its gaining ground upon him, he should, if within reach of fire-engines, keep everything close, and await their arrival, instead of admitting air to the fire by ineffectual efforts to oppose it with inadequate means. In the meantime, however, he should examine where a supply of water is most likely to be obtained, and communicate that, and any other local information, to the firemen on their coming forward. If there be no fire-engine within reach, the person who has examined the fire should keep the place where it is situated as close as possible, till as many buckets of water as can be easily collected are placed within his reach.

Taking care always that there is some one ready to assist him, he should then open the door, and creep forward on his hands and knees till he gets as near the fire as possible; holding his breath, and standing up for a moment to give the water a proper direction, he should throw it with force, using a hand pump if available, and instantly get down to his former position, where he will be again able to breathe. The people behind handing forward another bucket of water, he repeats the operation till the fire is quenched, or until he feels exhausted; in which case some one should take his place. If there be enough of water, however, two, three, or any convenient number of people may be employed in throwing it; on the contrary, if the supply of water be insufficient to employ even one person, the door should be kept shut while the water is being brought, and the air excluded as much as possible, as the fire burns exactly in proportion to the quantity of air which it receives.

One great evil, and which ought to be strictly guarded against by people not accustomed to fire, is, that on the first alarm they exert themselves to the very utmost of their strength. This, of course, can last but a short time; and when they feel tired, which in that case soon happens, they very often give up altogether. Now this is the reverse of what it ought to be. In extinguishing fires, like most other things, a cool judgment and steady perseverance are far more effective than any desultory exertions which can be made.

The heat generally increases in a considerable degree when water is first thrown upon a fire, from the conversion of a portion of it into steam. This is sometimes very annoying; so much so, that the persons engaged in throwing the water, frequently feel themselves obliged to give back a little. They should on no account, however, abate or discontinue their exertions in throwing the water with as much force as possible in the direction of the fire; it will in a short time cool the air and materials, and the steam will, in consequence, be generated more slowly, while a steady perseverance on the part of those employed can alone effect the object in view.

When water is scarce, mud, cow or horse dung, damp earth, &c., may be used as substitutes; but if there seems no chance of succeeding by any of these, and the fire is likely to extend to other buildings, the communication should be immediately cut off by pulling down the building next to that on fire. Any operation of this sort, however, should be begun at a sufficient distance from the fire to allow the communication to be completely cut off, before it gains upon the workmen. If this operation be attempted so near the fire as to be interrupted by it, it must be begun again at a greater distance; and, in that case, there is a greater destruction of property than might have been necessary.

If a fire occur in a stable or cow-house, surrounded with other buildings of the same description, or with the produce of a farm, there is much danger. The cattle and horses should be immediately removed; and, in doing so, if any of them become restive, they should be blindfolded, taking care that it is done thoroughly, as any attempt to blindfold them partially, only increases the evil. They should be handled as much as possible in the ordinary manner, and with great coolness; the violent gestures and excited appearance of the persons removing them tending greatly to startle the animals, and render them unmanageable.

PUBLIC FIRE BRIGADES AND THE DUTIES OF FIREMEN.

The best public means of arresting fires is a very wide question, as the only limit to the means is the expense. Different nations have different ways of doing the same thing. On the Continent generally, the whole is managed by Government, and the firemen are placed under martial law, the inhabitants being compelled to work the engines. In London, the principal means of arresting fires is a voluntary association of the insurance companies, without legal authority of any sort, the legal protection by parish engines being, with a few praiseworthy exceptions, a dead letter.

In Liverpool, Manchester, and other towns, the extinction of fires by the pressure of water only, without the use of fire-engines, is very much practised. The advantages of this system are very great; but, to enable us to follow this system in London, the whole water supply would require to be remodelled.

In America, the firemen are generally volunteers, enrolled by the local Governments. They are exempt from other duties, or are entitled to privileges, which appear to satisfy them, as the situation of fireman is eagerly sought in most of the American cities.

Which is the best of these different modes it is difficult to say; perhaps each is best suited for the place where it exists.

It is now generally admitted, that the whole force brought together to extinguish a fire ought to be under the direction and control of one individual. By this means, all quarrelling among the firemen about the supply of water, the interest of particular insurance companies, and other matters of detail, is avoided. By having the whole force under the command of one person, he is enabled to form one general plan of operations, to which the whole body is subservient; and although he may not, in the hurry of the moment, at all times adopt what will afterwards appear to be the best plan, yet it is better to have some general arrangement, than to allow the firemen of each engine to work according to their own fancy, and that, too, very often in utter disregard as to whether their exertions may aid or retard those of their neighbours. The individual appointed to such a situation ought not to be interfered with, or have his attention distracted, except by the chief authority on the spot, or the owner of the premises on fire. Much valuable information is frequently obtained from the latter, as to the division of the premises, the party-walls, and other matters connected with its locality. But, generally speaking, the less interference and advice the better, as it occupies time which may generally be better employed.

I need scarcely add, that on no account whatever should directions be given to the firemen by any other individual while the superintendent of brigade is present; and that there may be no quarrelling about superiority, the men should be aware on whom the command is to devolve in his absence.

It has often been to me a matter of surprise, that so small a portion of the public attention should be directed to the matter of extinguishing fires. It is only when roused by some great calamity that people bestir themselves; and then there is such a variety of plans proposed to avert similar cases of distress, that to attempt to concoct a rational plan out of such a crude, ill-digested, and contradictory mass of opinion, requires more labour and attention than most people are inclined to give it, unless a regular business was made of it. In Paris the corps of military firemen are so well trained, that although their apparatus is not so good as it should be, the amount of the losses by fire is comparatively trifling. If the head-quarters of such an establishment were to be in London, a store of apparatus, constructed on one uniform plan, could be kept there, to be forwarded to any other part of the kingdom where it might be required. This uniformity of the structure and design of the apparatus could extend to the most minute particulars; a screw or a nut of any one engine would fit every other engine in the kingdom. A depot could also be kept at head-quarters, where recruits would be regularly drilled and instructed in the business, and a regular system of communication kept up with all the provincial corps. Any particular circumstances occurring at a fire would thus be immediately reported, and the advantages of any knowledge or experience thus gained, would be disseminated over the whole kingdom. As the matter at present stands one town may have an excellent fire-engine establishment, and another within a few miles a very indifferent one, and when the one is called to assist the other, they can neither act in concert, nor can the apparatus of the one in case of accident be of the smallest service in replacing that of the other. The best might (if a proper communication were kept up) be under frequent obligations to the worst, and here, as in other matters, it is chiefly by communication that knowledge is increased. If the whole experience of the country were brought together, and maturely considered and digested by persons competent to judge, I have no doubt that a system might be introduced suitable to the nation and to the age in which we live. Instead of hearing of the "dreadful losses by fire," and the "great exertions" made to extinguish it, all the notice would be, such a place took fire, the engines arrived, and it was extinguished.

It would be useless for me to enter into the details of a plan which I have little hope of ever seeing realized. I may state, however, that a premium might be offered for the best engine of a size previously agreed upon, which, when finished, should be kept as a model.

Specifications could then be made out, and estimates advertised for, for all the different parts, such as wheels, axles, levers, cisterns, barrels, air-vessels, &c., separately. When any particular part of an engine was damaged, it could be immediately replaced, and the engine again rendered fit for service; and upon emergency any number of engines could be set up, merely by putting the different parts together. The work would also be better done; at least it would be much more easy to detect faults in the materials or workmanship than if the engines were bought ready for use. These remarks apply to all the rest of the apparatus.

It could be provided that firemen might be enlisted for a term of years. When enlisted, they would be sent to the depot at head-quarters, drilled to the use of the engines, and carefully instructed in separating and cleaning the different parts. Here also they could be practised in gymnastic exercises, and generally instructed in everything tending to promote their usefulness as firemen. They could then be sent off to some large towns, and, after having seen a little active service, distributed over the country in such parties as might be deemed necessary for the places they were intended to protect.

The practice of keeping fire-engines at noblemen's and gentlemen's residences, and at large manufactories in the country, is by no means uncommon, and I have no doubt that many more would supply themselves in this way if they knew where to apply for information in such matters; but the great fault lies in the want of persons of skill and experience to work them when fire occurs. In the way I have mentioned, proprietors and others could have one or more of their workmen instructed in this necessary piece of duty; and I have no doubt that many gentlemen would avail themselves of the means of instructing some of their servants.

It will be observed, I do not propose that the firemen who are enlisted, drilled, and instructed in the business, should be sent to the different stations in sufficient numbers to work the engines; this part of the work can be performed by any man accustomed to hard labour, as well as by the most expert fireman, and the local authorities could easily provide men for this purpose. In small towns, where fires are rare, the novelty would draw together plenty of hands; and in large towns, where the inhabitants are not sufficiently disinterested to work for nothing, there are always plenty who could be bound to assist in cases of fire at a certain rate per hour, to be paid upon a certificate from the fireman who has charge of the engine at which they worked. The trained firemen would thus be required only for the direction of the engine, attaching the hose, &c.

I am quite aware that many people object to the training of firemen; but it would be just as reasonable to give to a mob all the "materiel" of war, and next day expect it to act like a regular army, as to expect engines to be managed with any general prospect of success, unless the men are properly trained and prepared for the duty which is expected from them. Fire is both a powerful and an insidious enemy, and those whose business it is to attack it will best succeed when they have become skilful and experienced in the use of their arms.

It is quite obvious that a fire brigade, however complete in its apparatus and equipments, must depend for its efficiency on the state of training and discipline of the firemen. Wherever there is inexperience, want of co-operation, or confusion amongst them, the utmost danger is to be apprehended in the event of fire. It is amidst the raging of this destructive element, the terror and bustle of the inhabitants, that organization and discipline triumph, and it is there, too, that coolness and promptitude, steadiness and activity, fearlessness and caution, are peculiarly required; but, unfortunately, it is then also that they are most rarely exhibited.

There should not be less than five or six men attached to each engine, who should be properly instructed and drilled, to take charge of it, and to guide the people who work at the levers.

The person having the principal charge of the engines should frequently turn over in his mind what might be the best plan, in such and such circumstances, supposing a fire to take place. By frequently ruminating on the subject, he will find himself, when suddenly turned out of bed at night, much more fit for his task than if he had never considered the matter at all. Indeed he will frequently be surprised, when examining the premises afterwards (which he ought always to do, and mark any mistakes he may have committed), that he should have adopted the very best mode of extinguishing the fire, amid the noise, confusion, and the innumerable advices showered down on him, by all those who consider themselves qualified or entitled to give advice in such matters; a number, by the way, which sometimes includes no inconsiderable portion of the spectators. He should also make himself well acquainted with the different parts of the town in which he may be appointed to act, and notice the declivities of the different streets, &c. He will find this knowledge of great advantage.

Any buildings, supposed to be particularly dangerous, should be carefully examined, and all the different places where supplies of water can be obtained for them noticed.

A knowledge of the locality thus obtained will be found of great advantage in case of a fire breaking out. Indeed all firemen, especially those having the charge of engines, should be instructed carefully to examine and make themselves acquainted with the localities of their neighbourhood or district. Such knowledge will often prove valuable in emergencies; the proprietors or tenants of the property on fire being sometimes in such a state of alarm, that no distinct intelligence can be got from them.

When an engine is brought to a fire, it ought to be placed as nearly as possible in a straight line between the supply of water and the premises on fire; taking care, however, to keep at such a distance from the latter that the men who work the pumps may be in no danger from being scorched by the heat, or of being annoyed by the falling of water or burning materials. Running the engine close upon the fire serves no good purpose, except to shorten the quantity of hose that would otherwise be required. The addition of twenty or thirty feet of hose makes very little difference in the working of the engine, and, when compared with the disadvantage of the men becoming unsteady from the idea of personal danger, is not even to be named. Indeed, if the engine be brought too near the fire, there is danger of the men quitting the levers altogether. I may also add that, both for the safety of the hose and the convenience of the inhabitants, the engine should be kept out of the way of people removing furniture.

When the hose is attached and the engine filled with water, the man who holds the branch-pipe, accompanied by another, should get so near the fire, inside the house, that the water from the branch may strike the burning materials. If he cannot accomplish this standing, he must get down on his hands and knees and creep forward, those behind handing up the hose. A stratum of fresh air is almost always to be depended on from six to twelve inches from the floor, so that if the air be not respirable to a person standing upright, he should instantly get down. I have often observed this fact, which indeed is well known; but I once saw an example of it which appeared to me to be so striking, that I shall here relate it. A fire had broken out in the third floor of a house, and when I reached the top of the stair, the smoke was rolling in thick heavy masses, which prevented me from seeing six inches before me. I immediately got down on the floor; above which, for a space of about eight inches the air seemed to be remarkably clear and bright. I could distinctly see the feet of the tables and other furniture in the apartment; the flames in this space burning as vivid and distinct as the flame of a candle, while all above the smoke was so thick that the eye could not penetrate it. The fire had already burst through three out of five windows in the apartment, yet, when lying flat on the floor, no inconvenience was felt except from the heat.

When the fire has broken through a floor, the supply of air along that floor is not to be depended on--the fire drawing the principal supply of air from the apartments below.

When the two first firemen have gained a favourable position, they should keep it as long as they are able; and when they feel exhausted, the men behind them should take their place.

The great point to which everything ought to be made subservient is, that the water on its discharge from the branch-pipe should actually strike the burning materials. This cannot be too often or too anxiously inculcated on every one connected with a fire-engine establishment. Every other method not having this for its grand object, will, in nine cases out of ten, utterly fail; and upon the degree of attention paid to this point, depends almost entirely the question as to the amount of damage the fire will occasion.

When approaching a fire, it should always be done by the door, if possible. When this is attended to, it is much easier to shift the hose from one apartment to another; and the current of fresh air, entering by the door and proceeding along the passages, makes respiration easier and safer than elsewhere.

When entrance by the door is impracticable, and access is to be gained by a window, the flames frequently burst through in such a manner as to render advance in the first instance impossible. In that case, the branch should be pointed against the window, nearly in a perpendicular direction; the water striking the lintel, and falling all round inside the window, will soon extinguish the fire at that point sufficiently to render an entrance practicable.

The old plan of standing with the branch pipe in the street, and throwing the water into the windows is a very random way of going to work; and for my own part, although I have seen it repeatedly tried, I never saw it attended with success. Indeed it is hardly to be expected that water, thrown from the street into a room three or four storeys high, can have any impression on closets, presses, or passages, divided probably with brick partitions in the centre of the house. The circumstance of having engines at work on both sides of the house does not alter the case. The fire very often burns up through the centre, and frequently, when the space between the windows is large, along the front or back wall, till it arrives at the roof, which the water cannot touch on account of the slates or tiles. On the other hand, when the firemen enter the house, the fire is almost wholly under their command. And when it happens that there is any corner which the water cannot directly strike, the fire in it may often be extinguished by throwing the water against an opposite wall or partition, and trusting to the recoil to throw it to the point required.

When the water is thrown from the street, it is impossible to say whether it touches the parts on fire or not. No one can tell anything about it, except when the flame appears at the windows.

On going with the branch inside the house, besides the advantage of the water rushing directly from the hose upon the fire, there is a great saving in the article of water itself. The whole that is thrown by the engine is applied to the right purpose. No part of it is lost; that which does not strike the burning materials falls within the house; and, by soaking those parts on which it falls, prevents their burning so rapidly when the flames approach them.

If, on entering an apartment, it be found that the flames cover a considerable space, it is of advantage, in some instances, to place the point of the thumb in contact with the water at the nozzle of the branch. By this means the water may be spread to cover any space under twenty or thirty feet, according to the pressure applied.

While speaking of the mode of entering houses on fire, I may mention that I have tried several inventions for the purpose of elevating the branch pipe and hose to the level of a second or third story window. But these, although exceedingly ingenious, appear to me to rest on a principle entirely wrong; I mean that of throwing water on the fire from the outside of the building.

Independent altogether of a mistaken principle of usefulness, one insuperable objection to all these machines, is the difficulty of conveying them with the necessary celerity, and the impossibility of packing them on the engine in such a manner that it may be worked without their being taken off, as it seems to me that every description of apparatus which cannot be conveyed along with the engine, is likely to be left behind when most wanted. It is notorious that parish fire-ladders are, for this reason, seldom or never made use of.

Many people object to going inside a building on fire on account of the danger. It ought never to be forgotten, however, that the danger increases with the delay; and that although at first there may be no danger, if the opportunity is not promptly seized, it may become very considerable.

Several of the firemen have at different times fainted, or become stupefied, from the want of fresh air; but as no one is ever allowed to enter singly, they have been, in all cases, immediately observed by their comrades, and relieved.

Another objection has been raised in the alleged difficulty of persuading men to risk their lives in this manner for the small consideration which is allowed them. The truth is, that any persuasions I have had occasion to use, have been generally on the other side.

To hold the branch is considered the post of honour; and when two engines are working together, I have sometimes difficulty in preventing the men from pressing forward farther than is absolutely necessary. This forwardness is not the result of pecuniary reward for the increase of risk, but a spirit of emulation is at work, and the man entrusted with this duty, if found drawing back, would be completely disgraced.

A retreat should in all cases be kept open, to provide against any accident that may occur; and as this may be done in almost all cases by means so easy and simple, there can be no excuse for its omission. At the same time no one but an expert fireman should be permitted to enter where there is personal danger.

The danger to which firemen are most exposed is catching cold, from their being so frequently drenched with water, and from their exposure to the sudden alternations of heat and cold. A man is turned out of bed at midnight, and in a few minutes after quitting it he is exposed to the sharp air, perhaps, of a frosty winter night; running to the fire as fast as he can, he is, from the exercise, joined to the oppressive heat inside the place on fire, in a few minutes in a state of the most profuse perspiration; and, while in this state, he is almost certain to be soaked with cold water. The smoke is sometimes so thick, that he comes under the range of the branch of the engine without being aware of it till the water strikes him. If he escape this chance, the water rushing on some other object, recoils on him, and produces the same effect; and if the fire be in the roof of the apartment, he must lie down on his back on the floor, and in this manner gets completely steeped.

A bath of this sort is neither very safe nor pleasant; and the only preventive of injury to the health is to keep the men in constant motion. When they are allowed to stand still or sit down, the danger is considerable. When the fire is extinguished, or in two or three hours after its commencement, I make it a rule to give every man a dram of spirits. If it be necessary to leave an engine on the spot, those of the men who are to remain are sent home to change their clothes.

THE LONDON FIRE BRIGADE.

The London Fire Brigade now (January, 1861) consists of one superintendent, four foremen, each being appointed to a district consisting of a fourth part of London, which he never leaves except on some very pressing emergency, and who, in the absence of the superintendent, has the sole command of all engines, or firemen, within, or who may come within, his district; twelve engineers, ten sub-engineers, forty-seven senior firemen, and forty-three junior firemen: in all, one hundred and seventeen individuals. In addition, there are fifteen drivers and thirty-seven horses, all living at the several stations, and ready when required. There is also a supplementary force of four extra firemen, four drivers, and eight horses living at the stations, pursuing their usual avocations, and only paid by the Committee when required. The mechanical appliances consist of twenty-seven large engines drawn by horses, eight small engines drawn by hand, two floating-engines worked by steam, one of forty-horse power, and the other of eighty-horse power, one land steam fire-engine, and twenty-eight hand-pumps, one of the latter being carried on each engine. When an engine is sent to a fire, only four firemen and one driver accompany it. The levers are worked by the by-standers, who are paid one shilling for the first hour, and sixpence for each succeeding hour, besides refreshments. Upwards of six hundred assistants have been thus employed at one time. The principal protection of London against fire is entirely voluntary on the part of the insurance companies, to whom the above establishment belongs; there being no law in any shape whatever to control or sustain the brigade; and with the exception of some fifteen or twenty, the parish-engines are comparatively useless at a serious fire. It must not be omitted, that the greatest possible assistance is given to the firemen by the police, of whom there are about 7000, in keeping back the crowd, &c. The fire-offices look upon the whole as a matter of private business, so that the brigade is proportioned quite as must to the amount which the offices think it prudent to spend as to the size of the place. Paris, which is not half the size of London, and the buildings of which are much more substantial, has upwards of 800 firemen. It appears to me that any success which the brigade may have attained depends, in a great measure, on the liberal pay given, by which the best men for the purpose can be obtained, the favourable view in which the brigade is regarded by the public, and the willing and able assistance given by a numerous and perhaps the best police in existence.

The firemen in London being constantly employed on weekly wages, give their whole time to their employers, and are much more under command than where men are only occasionally employed. The wages and treatment being liberal, although the discipline is severe, there are generally a considerable number of candidates for each vacancy. Thus good men are obtained, seamen being preferred, as they are taught to obey orders, and the night and day watches and the uncertainty of the occupation are more similar to their former habits, than to those of other men of the same rank in life. The large number of fires is, however, the principal cause of any advantage the London firemen may possess over those of smaller places; and it is hardly fair to compare firemen who have only an opportunity of attending one or two fires in a week, to those who attend nearly three fires a day.

The firemen are drilled first daily, and then two or three times a week, for some months; and this, with an average of three calls a day, soon makes them acquainted with the routine of their business; but it takes years of constant work to make a thoroughly good fireman.

The management of the London Fire Brigade is confided to a Committee, consisting of one of the directors or secretaries from each of the fire-offices in London.

The superintendent has the command of the whole force.

The town is divided into four districts, in each of which there are stationed a sufficient number of engines, under the charge of a foreman, with engines and firemen under him.

The districts are as follows:--

NORTH SIDE OF RIVER.

District A. From the eastward to Paul's Chain, St. Paul's Churchyard, Aldersgate-street, and Goswell-street-road.

B. From St. Paul's, &c., to Tottenham-court-road, Crown-street, and St. Martin's-lane.

C. From Tottenham-court-road, &c., westward.

D. South side of River.

The men are clothed uniformly; are distinguished by numbers corresponding with their names in the books; and regularly exercised in the use of their engines, and in such other duties as the Committee or Superintendent may direct.

The following general regulations do not contain rules of conduct applicable to every variety of circumstance that may occur to individuals in the performance of their duty, as something must always be left for the exercise of intelligence and discretion; and, according to the degree in which these qualities in members of the Establishment are combined with zeal and activity, they become entitled to future promotion and reward.

It is strongly impressed upon the minds of all persons serving in the Establishment, that one of the greatest advantages which the present system possesses above that which it superseded, is derived from the embodying the whole force under one responsible officer. It is, therefore, incumbent upon the men to render prompt and cheerful obedience to the commands of their superiors; to execute their duties as steadily and quietly as possible; to be careful not to annoy the inhabitants of houses they may be called upon to enter, and to treat all persons with civility; to take care to preserve presence of mind and good temper, and not to allow themselves to be distracted from their duty by the advice or directions of any persons but their own officers, and to observe the strictest sobriety and general regularity of behaviour.

As every man wears the uniform of the Establishment, which is marked with a number corresponding with his name in the books, he must constantly bear in mind that misconduct will not only reflect discredit upon the Establishment, but be easily brought home to himself and subject him to proportional punishment.

The men are particularly cautioned not to take spirituous liquors from any individual without special permission of the superintendent, or, in his absence, of the foreman of the district; and as intoxication upon the alarming occasion of fires is not only disreputable to the Establishment, but in the highest degree dangerous, by rendering the men unfit for duty, every appearance of it is most rigidly marked, and the foremen, engineers, and sub-engineers report immediately, for the purpose of being laid before the Committee, every instance of insubordination or intoxication, and the men are accordingly apprised that the regulations regarding the above-mentioned faults will be most strictly enforced.

All the men in the Establishment are liable to be punished by fine, suspension, reduction, or dismissal, for disobeying or neglecting any of these regulations, or for any other misconduct; and the disposal of the fines so collected is at the discretion of the Committee.

The following are the conditions upon which each man is admitted into the Establishment:--

He devotes his whole time to the service.

He serves and resides wherever he is appointed.

He must promptly obey all orders which he may receive from those placed in authority over him.

The age of admission does not exceed twenty-five, nor is under eighteen.

He conforms himself to all regulations which may be made from time to time.

He does not upon any occasion, or under any pretence whatever, take money from any person, without the express permission of the Committee.

He appears at all times in the dress of the Establishment.

If lodgings be found for him, a deduction of one shilling per week is made from his pay, if unmarried; if married, and if lodgings be found for him, an agreement in each particular case will be made.

He receives his pay weekly on such day as shall be appointed.

The pay of a Junior Fireman is 3s. per day, or 21s. a week.

The pay of a Senior Fireman, 3s. 6d. a day, or 24s. 6d. a week.

The pay of a Sub-Engineer is 26s. a week.

The pay of an Engineer, 4s. a day, or 28s. a week.

The Foremen are paid by annual salaries.

Each man contributes towards a Superannuation Fund, according to a scale determined by the Committee.

Each man receives annually--

One short frock coat, marked with a number answering to his name in the books.

A black neckcloth.

Two pairs of cloth trousers.

One cloth cap.

Four pairs of boots in three years, and

Once in three years he receives--

One great coat.

He does not quit the service without giving fourteen days' previous notice; if he quits without such notice, or is dismissed, the whole of his pay then due is forfeited.

Every man who is dismissed from the Establishment, or who resigns his situation, delivers up, before he quits the service, every article of dress and appointment which may have been supplied to him; if any of such articles have been, in the opinion of the superintendent, improperly used or damaged, the man makes good the damage or supplies a new article.

Every man in the service is liable to immediate dismissal for unfitness, negligence, or misconduct. The Committee, if they see fit, may dismiss a man without assigning any reason.

No fireman must allow to be used by any other person, nor use himself, except while he belongs to the Establishment, the button and badge given with his clothes.

In the event of sickness rendering any man incapable of performing his duties, the Committee reserves to itself the power of making a deduction from his weekly pay.

Each man, on his admission, gives to the Committee, if required, a letter of guarantee from some respectable person, to an amount not exceeding 50l., as security.

OUTLINE OF GENERAL DUTY.

One-third of the men are constantly on duty at the different engine-houses, night and day; and the whole are liable to be called up for attendance at fires, or for any other duty. In general, it is arranged as follows, viz.:--

If a fire happen in District A, the whole of the men and engines of that district immediately repair to the spot; two-thirds of the men, and one of the engines, from each of the districts B and D, also go to the fire; and one-third of the men from the district C.

If the fire happen in B, the whole of the men and engines in that district immediately repair to the fire; one engine from A, another from C, two-thirds of the men from A and C, and one-third of the men from D.

If the fire happen in C, the whole of the men and engines in that district, one engine and two-thirds of the men from the district B, and one-third of the men from A and D, go to the fire.

If the fire happen in D, the whole of the men and engines in that district, with one engine and two-thirds of the men from the district A, and one-third of the men from B and C, shall go to the fire.

If a fire happen on the boundary of a district, and it is doubtful in which district it has occurred, the whole of the engines and men of the two adjoining districts instantly proceed to the spot, and one-third of the men of the two remaining districts.

In case of emergency, the superintendent calls in such additional force as he may require.

The engines are not taken to alarms of chimneys on fire, unless the circumstances of the case should, in the opinion of the superintendent, foreman, or engineer, require a deviation from this regulation.

When any of the men from another district come to assist at a fire, if the engine to which they are attached is not in attendance, they instantly go to the foreman's engine of the district to which they come.

The engines are conveyed to fires at not less than seven miles per hour, and the men who do not accompany the engines go at not less than four miles per hour.

Any engineer or fireman who, when at a fire, is absent from an engine or a branch pipe, without orders from the superintendent or foreman, is liable to a fine.

If any of the men are sick, or absent from any other cause, their duties are performed by other men attached to their engine-station.

With a view to the men being always at hand, they are lodged as near as possible to their respective engine-houses.

The roll is called at each station every morning and evening.

No man leaves his own residence or the engine-station to which he belongs from 10 P.M. to 6 A.M. except to go to a fire, or by an order from a superior, or with written leave from the superintendent, and the senior man on duty is answerable if he does not report any departure from this rule.

Men on duty not at the engine-stations are allowed one hour for breakfast and one for dinner, as follows:--One-half of the men on duty go to breakfast from 8 to 9, and the other half from 9 to 10; also one-half go to dinner from 1 to 2, and the other half from 2 to 3. The second half in no case leave until the whole of the first half have returned, neither do the men on duty leave morning or evening until the relief has arrived. The engineer or senior man on duty is answerable for this regulation being carried into effect. And any man being absent from the premises he is watching or working in, except at the regular hours, is punished.

The men for duty individually assemble at the principal engine-house in the district before, or precisely at, the hour fixed for that purpose. Their names are called, and an inspection made by the foreman of the district, to ascertain that they are sober and correctly dressed and appointed. The foreman then reads and explains the orders of the day. At the hour for relieving the men, no one leaves his engine-house until the relief has actually arrived there; when the men are relieved, their names are called over, and they are inspected by the engineer, that he may ascertain whether they are sober, and as correctly dressed and appointed as when they went on duty. The engineer enters these inspections in a book.

The engineers deliver a written report, according to a printed form, twice each day, to the foreman of the district, who in his turn reports twice a day to the superintendent.

The whole of the men are, at all times, ready to appear at any place required, for exercise or any other purpose, and are ready (whether on duty or not) to execute whatever orders they may receive, in relation to the Establishment, from the engineers, foremen, or superintendent.

DUTIES OF SUPERINTENDENT.

The Superintendent resides at the principal engine-station in Watling-street.

The moment an alarm of fire is given, wherever it may be, he repairs to the spot with all possible expedition, and takes the command of the whole force.

He endeavours to ascertain the cause of the fire, and reports the same to the committee.

He is responsible for the general conduct of the foremen, engineers, and firemen under his charge.

He makes himself well acquainted with the character and conduct of every man under his orders.

He must be firm and just, and, at the same time, kind and conciliating in his behaviour on all occasions.

He takes care that the printed regulations and all others given out from time to time, are promptly and strictly obeyed; and he gives clear and precise instructions to the men under him, and reports every instance of neglect of a serious nature to the Committee.

He must feel the importance of visiting some of the engine-houses, at uncertain hours, every day and night.

He suspends and reports to the Committee persons who are guilty of serious misconduct; and at once punishes by fines, according to a scale sanctioned by the Committee, irregularities of a lighter character, reporting such fines to them.

He must be at all times prepared to furnish the Committee with particulars respecting the state of the Establishment.

When a fire is extinguished, the superintendent retains only such a number of men and engines as he may think necessary for watching the premises.

He communicates with the surveyors of stock of the offices interested in a fire, and arranges with them, in the event of its being necessary, to work out salvage from the ruins.

When a fire happens, he causes a report to be made immediately, if in office hours (or, if after office hours, before ten o'clock next morning), to those offices interested in the fire, and also to their surveyors of buildings and stock, as soon as possible after the fire is extinguished, and causes a daily report to be transmitted to each office of all fires which have happened, according to a printed form given to him for that purpose, as follows:--

Date and hour.

Situation of premises.

Name and occupation of tenant.

Name and residence of landlord.

Supposed cause of fire.

In what offices insured.

No. of Policy.

If there is gas on the premises.

By whom called.

By whom extinguished.

Supply of water, with name of company.

No. of engines attending and of what district, and the order in which they arrive.

No. of men ditto ditto.

Engines not of the Establishment, and the order in which they arrive.

Description of damage.

DUTIES OF FOREMAN.

The Foreman resides at the place appointed for him.

He receives his orders and instructions from, and makes his reports to, the superintendent.

He must set an example to the men of alacrity and skill in the discharge of his duty, and of regularity in his general behaviour.

In the absence of the superintendent, the foreman of the district will take the command of the whole force, both those of his own district and of all other engines and men which may come to his assistance in cases of fire.

He does not attend fires that happen out of his own district unless he receives orders from the superintendent to that effect.

He endeavours to ascertain the cause of the fire, and reports the same to the superintendent.

On the alarm of fire being given in his own district, he instantly repairs to the spot, and uses his utmost endeavours to get the engines into play and supply them with water. The first engine and firemen which arrive at a fire are not interfered with, nor their supplies of water diverted from them, by those coming afterwards, unless by a distinct order from the superintendent, or, in his absence, from the foreman of the district. The same rule applies to each succeeding engine which takes up a position.

He is careful to place the engines in such a manner that the men who work at the levers may be in no danger from the falling of the premises on fire; and also that the engines may not be in the way of people carrying out furniture, &c.; but, above all things, he endeavours to place the engineers with their branch pipes in such positions that the water from the branches may directly strike the burning materials. This he cannot too often inculcate on the men placed under him, as upon this point, on being properly attended to, depends entirely the effect of the engines. To attain this most desirable end, it is frequently necessary to enter the premises on fire, and the foreman takes care so to place his men that they can easily escape. If he has reason to suspect that the building is not sufficiently secure, he stations one or two competent men to observe the state of the building, and to give the alarm when they see any danger.

He never allows any man unaccompanied by another to enter a building on fire.

He does not throw more water on the premises than is absolutely necessary to extinguish the fire, as all the water thrown after the fire is extinguished, only tends to increase the damage.

When the inmates of the premises on fire are removed, the foreman endeavours to exclude air from the parts on fire, by shutting all doors and windows as far as may be practicable.

He is responsible for the conduct of the men placed under him, and for the state of the engines, which must at all times be kept in first-rate order; he also makes himself well acquainted with the talent and general character of each individual under him.

He visits every engine-house in his district at least once in the twenty-four hours; he sees that the men are on duty, the engines ready for service, and everything in proper order, and enters his visit in a book kept for that purpose, with the date and hour of his visit. If he finds anything wrong, he enters it in the book, and immediately sends off a report to the superintendent by one of the men not on duty.

He sends a written report twice in every twenty-four hours to the superintendent, which contains a particular statement of all fires and everything else connected with the Establishment which has occurred in his district within the preceding twelve hours.

He returns in his report of a fire the names of such men, if any, as were not ready to start with the engine to which they are attached.

It is expected that he is able and ready to give instructions to the engineers and men on all points relating to their duty.

He receives and enters, in a book kept for that purpose, all complaints which may be made against any person under his command, causing the complaining party to sign the same and insert his address, and he reports the whole matter without delay to the superintendent.

He is responsible for the engines in his district being each provided with the articles contained in the following list:--

2 lengths of scaling ladder.

1 canvas sheet, with 10 or 12 handles of rope round the edge of it, used as a portable fire-escape.

2 pieces of 2-1/2-inch rope, one 10 fathoms and one 14 fathoms long.

7 lengths of hose, each 40 feet long.

2 branch pipes, one 4 and the other 1 foot long.

3 nozzles, or jet pipes.

4 lengths of suction-pipe, each about 6 feet long.

1 flat rose.

1 standcock.

1 goose-neck.

2 balls of strips of sheep-skin.

2 balls of small cord.

4 hose wrenches.

1 fire hook.

1 mattock.

1 shovel.

1 saw.

1 screw-wrench.

1 portable cistern.

1 hatchet or pole-axe.

1 iron crow-bar.

DUTIES OF THE ENGINEER.

He resides in the engine-house to which he is appointed.

He obeys all orders given to him by the superintendent or the foreman of the district.

He must set an example to the men of alacrity and skill in the discharge of his duty, and of regularity in his general behaviour.

He is held responsible for the conduct of the men under him, and for the state of his engine, and takes care that it is provided with the articles contained in the foregoing list.

He reports to his foreman, every morning and evening, in writing, whether any of his men have been absent with or without leave.

He enters in his book the time when the men go to the foreman's station before taking duty, and also when they return.

On receiving notice of a fire happening within the prescribed limits, he instantly takes his engine and men to the spot, and places himself and them at the disposal of the superintendent, foreman, or senior engineer of the district in which the fire happens.

He must make himself acquainted with the character and abilities of each man under him.

He is subject to fines at the discretion of the Committee, for neglect of duty or misbehaviour.

DUTIES OF SUB-ENGINEERS.

The sub-engineers being attached to foremen's and double stations only, in the absence of the foremen or engineer, or when in charge of an engine, the duties of the sub-engineer are the same as those described for an engineer; when the foreman or engineer is absent, the sub-engineer must set an example to the firemen at the station of constant attention, implicit obedience and activity, and in so far as he exhibits these and similar qualifications he expects to rise in the service.

DUTIES OF THE FIREMAN.

Every fireman in the establishment may expect to rise to the superior stations, by activity, intelligence, sobriety, and general good conduct.

He must make it his study to recommend himself to notice by a diligent discharge of his duties, and strict obedience to the commands of his superiors, recollecting that he who has been accustomed to obey will be considered best qualified to command.

He resides near the engine-house to which he is attached, in a situation to be approved of, and devotes the whole of his time and abilities to the service.

On the alarm of fire, he proceeds with all possible speed to the engine-house to which he is attached.

He must at all times appear neat in his person, and correctly dressed in the establishment uniform, and be respectful in his demeanour towards his superiors.

He must readily and punctually obey the orders of the engineers, foremen, and superintendent.

He must not quit his engine-house while on duty, except to go to a fire, unless by special order from a superior.

He is subject to fines for neglect of duty or misbehaviour, according to the regulations.

BOOKS KEPT AT THE STATIONS.

There is a book kept in each engine-house, in which are entered all fires or alarms of fires; the time the men come on duty; the visits made by the foremen, superintendent, or any of the Committee, and all complaints against the men.

This book is in charge of the superior on duty at the time; and the foreman and engineers are answerable for its being correctly kept.

Every entry made in this book is signed by the person making it.

The superintendent enters, in a book kept for that purpose, the particulars of every fire, the attendance of engines, supply of water, &c., and lays it before the Committee weekly, or oftener, if required.

Any false entry, for the purpose of concealing absence, is punished--for the first offence, by the reduction of one step, and for the second by dismissal.

FOOTNOTES:

[Footnote F: At a fire which took place in one of the best streets in Edinburgh, and which began in the roof, the persons who rushed into the house on the first alarm being given, threw the greater part of the contents of the drawing-room and library, with several basketsful of china and glass, out of the windows; the fire injured nothing below the uppermost story.]

THE EDINBURGH FIRE BRIGADE.

In forming the brigade in Edinburgh, where the firemen are only occasionally employed, the description of men, from which I made a selection, were slaters, house-carpenters, masons, plumbers, and smiths.

Slaters make good firemen, not so much from their superiority in climbing, going along roofs, &c., although these are great advantages, but from their being in general possessed of a handiness and readiness which I have not been able to discover in the same degree amongst other classes of workmen. It is, perhaps, not necessary that I should account for this, but it appears to me to arise from their being more dependent on their wits, and more frequently put to their shifts in the execution of their ordinary avocations. House-carpenters and masons being well acquainted with the construction of buildings, and understanding readily from whence danger is to be apprehended, can judge with tolerable accuracy, from the appearance of a house, where the stair is situated, and how the house is divided inside. Plumbers are also well accustomed to climbing and going along the roofs of houses; they are useful in working fire-cocks, covering the gratings of drains with lead, and generally in the management of water. Smiths and plumbers can also better endure heat and smoke than most other workmen.

Men selected from these five trades are also more robust in body, and better able to endure the extremes of heat, cold, wet, and fatigue, to which firemen are so frequently exposed, than men engaged in more sedentary employments.

I have generally made it a point to select for firemen, young men from seventeen or eighteen to twenty-five years of age. At that age they enter more readily into the spirit of the business, and are much more easily trained, than when farther advanced in life. Men are frequently found who, although they excel in the mechanical parts of their own professions, are yet so devoid of judgment and resources, that when anything occurs which they have not been taught, or have not been able to foresee, they are completely at a loss. Now it happens not unfrequently that the man who arrives first at a fire, notwithstanding any training or instructions he may have received, is still, from the circumstances of the case, left almost entirely to the direction of his own judgment. It is, therefore, of immense importance to procure men on whose coolness and judgment you can depend. If they are expert tradesmen, so much the better, as there is generally a degree of respect shown to first-rate tradesmen by their fellows, which inferior hands can seldom obtain; and this respect tends greatly to keep up the character of the corps to which they belong, which ought never to be lost sight of.

Amidst the noise and confusion which more or less attend all fires, I have found considerable difficulty in being able to convey the necessary orders to the firemen in such a manner as not to be liable to misapprehension. I tried a speaking-trumpet; but, finding it of no advantage, it was speedily abandoned. It appeared to me indeed, that while it increased the sound of the voice, by the deep tone which it gave, it brought it into greater accordance with the surrounding noise. I tried a boatswain's call, which I have found to answer much better. Its shrill piercing note is so unlike any other sound usually heard at a fire, that it immediately attracts the attention of the firemen. By varying the calls, I have now established a mode of communication not easily misunderstood, and sufficiently precise for the circumstances to which it is adapted, and which I now find to be a very great convenience.

The calls are as follows:--

1 for red, 2 for blue, 3 for yellow, 4 for grey.[G]

5 to work the engine.

6 to stop working.

7 to attach one length of hose more than the engine has at the time the call is given.

8 to coil up the hose attached to the engine.

9 to coil up the hose attached to the fire-cock.

10 to turn to the left.

11 to turn to the right.

12 the call to work the engine answers also to move forward when the engine is prepared for travelling.

13 the call to stop working answers to stop the engine when moving forward.

In all there are thirty-six calls when compounded with the first four.

In speaking of the drilling of firemen, I shall give a short account of the plan followed here, which has been tolerably successful.

The present number of firemen in Edinburgh is fifty, divided into four companies; three of which consist of twelve and one of fourteen men. The bounds of the city are divided into four districts; in each of which there is an engine-house, containing one or more engines, one of the companies being attached to each engine-house. In each company there is one captain, one sergeant, four pioneers, and six or eight firemen.

The whole are dressed in blue jackets, canvas trousers, and hardened leather helmets, having hollow leather crests over the crown to ward off falling materials. The form of this helmet was taken from the war-helmet of the New Zealanders, with the addition of the hind flap of leather to prevent burning matter, melted lead, water, or rubbish getting into the neck of the wearer. The captains' helmets have three small ornaments, those of the sergeants one--those of the pioneers and firemen being plain.

The jackets of the captains have two small cloth wings on the shoulder, similar to those worn by light infantry. Those of the sergeants have three stripes on the left arm, and, on the left arms of the pioneers and firemen, are their respective numbers in the company. Each company has a particular colour--red, blue, yellow, and grey. Each engine is painted of one or other of these colours, and the accoutrements of the men belonging to it correspond. There is thus no difficulty in distinguishing the engines or men from each other by their colours and numbers. Each man also wears a broad leather waist-belt, with a brass buckle in front. To the waist-belts of the captains, sergeants, and pioneers is attached eighty feet of cord; the captains having also a small mason's hammer, with a crow-head at the end of the handle: the sergeants have a clawed hammer, such as is used by house-carpenters, with an iron handle, and two openings at the end for unscrewing nuts from bolts; the pioneers a small hatchet, with a crow-head at the end of the handle; and the firemen each carry a canvas water-bucket folded up.

The captains assemble every Tuesday night, to give in a report of such fires as may have occurred in their respective districts, with a list of the men who have turned out, and a corresponding list from the sergeant of police of the respective districts. They then receive any orders which may be necessary; and any vacancies which have occurred in the establishment are filled up at these meetings.

For some months after this fire establishment was organized, the men were regularly drilled once a week, at four o'clock in the morning; but now only once a month at the same hour.

Among many other good reasons for preferring this early hour, I may mention, that it does not interfere with the daily occupation of the firemen. The chance of collecting a crowd is also avoided, as there are then comparatively few people on the streets; this is a matter of some importance, as a crowd of people not only impedes the movements of the firemen, but, from small quantities of water spilt on the by-standers, quarrels are generated, and a prejudice excited against the corps, to avoid which every exertion should be used to keep the firemen on good terms with the populace.

The mornings, too, at this early hour, are dark for more than half the year, and the firemen are thus accustomed to work by torch-light, and sometimes without any light whatever, except the few public lamps which are then burning. And, as most fires happen in the night, the advantage of drilling in the dark must be sufficiently obvious.

The inhabitants have sometimes complained of being disturbed with the noise of the engines at so early an hour; but when the object has been explained, they have generally submitted, with a good grace, to this slight evil. A different part of the city being always chosen for each successive drill, the annoyance occasioned to any one district is very trifling, and of very unfrequent occurrence.

On the Tuesday evening preceding the drill, the captains are informed when and where the men are to assemble. These orders they communicate to the individual firemen. A point of rendezvous being thus given to the whole body, every man, who is not on the spot at the hour appointed, fully equipped, with his clothes and accoutrements in good order, is subjected to a fine. Arrived on the ground, the men are divided into two parties, each party consisting of two companies, that being the number required to work each large engine without any assistance from the populace. The whole are then examined as to the condition of their clothing and equipments.

The captains, sergeants, and pioneers of each company alternately take the duty of directing the engine, attaching the hose, &c., while the whole of each party not engaged in these duties take the levers as firemen. The call is then given to move forward, the men setting off at a quick walking pace, and, on the same call being repeated, they get into a smart trot. When the call to stop is given, with orders to attach one or more lengths of hose to the engine and fire-cock, it is done in the following manner:--No. 1 takes out the branch pipe, and runs out as far as he thinks the hose ordered to be attached will reach, and there remains; No. 2 takes a length of hose out of the engine, and uncoils it towards No. 1; and No. 3 attaches the hose to the engine. If more than one length is required, No. 4 takes out another, couples it to the former length, and then uncoils it. If a third length is wanted, No. 3 comes up with it, after having attached the first length to the engine. If more lengths are still wanted, No: 2 goes back to the engine for another; Nos. 3 and 4 follow, and so on till the requisite length is obtained; No. 1 then screws on the branch-pipe at the farther extremity of the last length.[H] While Nos. 1, 2, 3, and 4 are attaching the hose to the engine, No. 5 opens the fire-cock door, screws on the distributor, and attaches the length of hose, which No. 6 uncoils; Nos. 7 and 8 assist, if more than one length of hose be required. Immediately on the call being given to attach the hose, the sergeant locks the fore-carriage of the engine, and unlocks the levers. The fire-cock being opened by No. 5 (who remains by it as long as it is being used), the sergeant holds the end of the hose which supplies the engine, and at the same time superintends the men who work the levers. The call being given to work the engine, the whole of the men, Nos. 1, 2, 3, 4, and 5, the captain and sergeant excepted, work at the levers along with the men of the other company.

Although these operations may appear complicated, they are all completed, and the engine in full play, with three lengths, or 120 feet of hose, in one minute and ten seconds, including the time required for the water to fill the engine so far as to allow it to work.

In order to excite a spirit of emulation, as well as to teach the men dexterity in working the engines, I frequently cause a competition amongst them. They are ordered to attach one or more lengths of hose to each of two engines, and to work them as quickly as possible, the first engine which throws water being considered the winner. They are sometimes also placed at an equal distance from each of two separate fire-cocks; on the call being given to move forward, each party starts for the fire-cock to which it is ordered, and the first which gets into play is of course held to have beat the other. The call to stop is then given, and both parties return to their former station, with their hose coiled up, and everything in proper travelling order; the first which arrives being understood to have the advantage.

The men are also carefully and regularly practised in taking their hose up common-stairs, drawing them up by ropes on the outside, and generally in accustoming themselves to, and providing against, every circumstance which may be anticipated in the case of fire.

When a fire occurs in a common-stair, the advantages arising from this branch of training are incalculable. The occupants, in some cases amounting to twenty or thirty families, hurrying out with their children and furniture, regardless of everything except the preservation of their lives and property, and the rush of the crowd to the scene of alarm, form altogether, notwithstanding the exertions of an excellent police, such a scene of confusion as those only who have witnessed it can imagine; and here it is that discipline and unity of purpose are indispensable; for, unless each man has already been taught and accustomed to the particular duty expected from him, he only partakes of the general alarm, and adds to the confusion. But even when a hose has been carried up the interior of a common-stair, the risk of damage from the people carrying out their furniture is so great, that the hose is not unfrequently burst, almost as soon as the engine has begun to play. If the hose be carried up to the floor on fire by the outside, the risk of damage is comparatively small, the hose in that case being only exposed for a short distance in crossing the stair.

During a period of four years the only two firemen who lost their lives were run down by their own engines; and, in order to avoid danger from this cause, they are frequently accustomed suddenly to stop the engines when running down the steep streets with which this city abounds. It is a highly necessary exercise, and is done by wheeling the engine smartly round to the right or left, which has the effect of immediately stopping its course.

There is a branch of training which I introduced amongst the Edinburgh firemen some time ago, which has been attended with more important advantages than was at first anticipated. I mean the gymnastic exercises. The men are practised in these exercises (in a small gymnasium fitted up for them in the head engine-house) regularly once a-week, and in winter sometimes twice: attendance on their part is entirely voluntary; the best gymnasts (if otherwise equally qualified) are always promoted in cases of vacancy.

So sensible were the Insurance Companies doing business here, of the advantages likely to arise from the practice of these exercises, that on one occasion they subscribed upwards of 10l., which was distributed in medals and money among the most expert and attentive gymnasts of the corps, at a competition in presence of the magistrates, commissioners of police, and managers of insurance companies.

Amongst the many advantages arising from these exercises I shall notice only one or two. The firemen, when at their ordinary employments, as masons, house-carpenters, &c., being accustomed to a particular exercise of certain muscles only, there is very often a degree of stiffness in their general movements, which prevents them from performing their duty as firemen with that ease and celerity which are so necessary and desirable; but the gymnastic exercises, by bringing all the muscles of the body into action, and by aiding the more general development of the frame, tend greatly to remove or overcome this awkwardness. But its greatest advantage is the confidence it gives to the men when placed in certain situations of danger. A man, for example, in the third or fourth floor of a house on fire, who is uncertain as to his means of escape, in the event of his return by the stair being cut off, will not render any very efficient service in extinguishing the fire; his own safety will be the principal object of his attention, and till that is to a certain extent secured, his exertions are not much to be relied upon. An experienced gymnast, on the other hand, placed in these circumstances, finds himself in comparative security. With a hatchet and eighty feet of cord at his command, and a window near him, he knows there is not much difficulty in getting to the street; and this confidence not only enables him to go on with his duty with more spirit, but his attention not being abstracted by thoughts of personal danger, he is able to direct it wholly to the circumstances of the fire. He can raise himself on a window sill, or the top of a wall, if he can only reach it with his hands; and by his hands alone he may sustain himself in situations where other means of support are unattainable, till the arrival of assistance. These are great advantages; but, as I said before, the greatest of all is that feeling of safety with which it enables a fireman to proceed with his operations, uncertainty or distraction being the greatest of possible evils. The cord carried at the waist-belt of the captains, sergeants, and pioneers, being fully sufficient to sustain a man's weight, and with the assistance of their small hatchets easily made fast, and the pioneers always being two together, there is thus no difficulty in descending even from a height of eighty feet: the cords should be doubled by way of security.

I.--GENERAL REGULATIONS OF THE EDINBURGH FIRE BRIGADE.

A list of the engine-houses, and the residences of the superintendent and head enginemen in each district shall be publicly advertised, that no one may be ignorant where to apply in cases of fire; and, in the event of fire breaking out in any house, the possessor shall be bound to give instant notice of it at the nearest station; and shall take particular care to keep all doors and windows shut in the premises where the fire happens to be.

"Fire-engine house" shall be painted in large characters on one or more prominent places of each engine-house; and the residences of the master of engines, head enginemen, inspectors of gas companies, and water-officers of the district, shall likewise be marked there.

The head enginemen and firemen shall reside as near the engine-house as possible.

As, in the case of a fire breaking out, it may be necessary to break open the doors of houses and shops in the neighbourhood, in order to prevent the fire from spreading, it is ordered, that no possessors of houses or shops in the neighbourhood shall go away, after the fire has broken out, without leaving the key of their house or shop, as otherwise the door will be broken open, if necessary; and it is recommended that all possessors of shops shall have the place of their residence painted upon their shop-doors, that notice may be sent them when necessary.

II.--POLICE.

Upon any watchman discovering fire, he shall call the neighbouring watchmen to his assistance--shall take the best means in his power to put all concerned upon their guard--and shall immediately send off notice to the nearest office and engine-house. The watchman, who is despatched to give these intimations, shall run as far as he can, and shall then send forward any other watchman whom he may meet, he himself following at a walk to communicate his information, in case of any mistake on the part of the second messenger.

Upon intimation of a fire being received at the main office, or a district office, the head officer on duty shall instantly give notice thereof to the head engineman of the district, to the master of engines, to the water-officers of the district, and to the inspectors of the different gas-light companies, and shall have power, if his force at the office at the time be deficient, to employ the nearest watchmen for these purposes; and, on intimation being first received at a district-office, the officer on duty in the office shall immediately send notice to the main office.

Upon intimation being received at the main office, the officer on duty shall also instantly send notice to the superintendent of police, and the lieutenants not at the office at the time--to the master of engines; to the head enginemen of the various districts; to the superintendent of the water company; to the lord provost or chief magistrate for the time; to the sheriff of the county; to the bailie residing nearest the place; to the dean of guild; to the members of fire-engine committee of commissioners of police; to the moderator of the high constables; and also to the managers of the different gaslight companies.

The officer on duty at the main office shall, with the least possible delay, send off to the fire a party of his men, under the command of a lieutenant or other officer.

This party, on arriving at the spot, shall clear off the crowd, and keep open space and passages for the firemen and others employed.

The officer commanding this party of the police shall attend to no instructions except such as he shall receive from the acting chief magistrate attending; or, in absence of a magistrate, from any member of the committee on fire-engines; and the men shall attend to the instructions of their own officer alone.

Three or more policemen shall be in attendance upon the acting chief magistrate and fire-engine committee; two policemen shall constantly attend the master of the engines, to be at his disposal entirely; and one policeman shall attend with the water-officer at each fire-cock that may be opened.

The superintendent of police shall always have a list of extra policemen hung up in the police-office, who, upon occasions of fire, may be called out, if necessary, and twenty of these extra men shall always be called out upon notice of fire being received at the main office, for the purpose of attending at the police-office, and rendering assistance where it may be required. The superintendent shall likewise have a supply of fire-buckets, flambeaux, and lanterns, at the office, to be ready when wanted.

There shall be no ringing of alarm-bells, beating of drums, or springing of rattles, except by written order from the chief magistrate for the time; but the alarm may be given by despatching messengers, with proper badges, through different parts of the town, when considered necessary.

III. SUPERINTENDENT OF FIRE BRIGADE.

On receiving notice of a fire, the superintendent shall instantly equip himself in his uniform, and repair to the spot where the fire is.

The necessary operations to be adopted shall be under his absolute control, and he will issue his instructions to the head enginemen and firemen.

The superintendent shall report from time to time to the chief magistrate in attendance (through such medium as may be at his command, but without his leaving the spot), the state of the fire, and whether a greater number of policemen, or a party of the military, be required, and anything else which may occur to him; and the master shall observe the directions of the chief magistrate attending, and those of no other person whatever.

The superintendent shall frequently inspect the engines, and all the apparatus connected therewith; he shall be responsible for the whole being at all times in good order and condition; and he shall have a general muster and inspection at least once every three months, when the engines and all the apparatus shall be tried. He shall also instruct the enginemen, firemen, and the watchmen, to unlock the plates, and screw on the distributors of the fire-cocks, or open the fire-plugs.

Whenever any repairs or new apparatus shall appear to be necessary, the superintendent shall give notice to the clerk of the police, whose duty it shall be instantly to convene the committee on fire-engines.

Upon a fire breaking out, the superintendent shall lose as little time as possible in stationing chimney-sweepers on the roofs of the adjoining houses, to keep them clear of flying embers; and also persons in each flat of the adjoining houses, to observe their state, and report if any appearances of danger should arise; such persons taking as much care as possible to keep all doors and windows of said flats shut, and the doors and windows of the premises where the fire happens to be shall, so far as practicable, be carefully kept shut.

The superintendent shall forthwith prepare regulations for the firemen, &c., under his charge, and report the same to the committee on fire-engines for their approval. Every fireman shall be furnished with a copy of such regulations, and shall be bound to make himself master of its contents; and it shall be the duty of the superintendent to see that the instructions are duly attended to in training and exercising the men.

IV.--HEAD ENGINEMEN.

Each head engineman shall attend to the engines placed in his district, and all the apparatus connected therewith, and report to the superintendent when any repairs or new apparatus seem requisite, and shall be responsible for the engines being in proper working condition at all times.

Upon receiving notice of a fire, the head enginemen shall call out the firemen in their respective districts; and they shall all repair, perfectly equipped, with the utmost expedition, to the spot where the fire happens to be, carrying along with them the engines and apparatus.

The head enginemen shall have the carts and barrels attached to their several districts always in readiness, in good order, and the barrels filled with water, which shall accompany the engines to the fire.

On arriving at the spot, the head enginemen shall take their instructions from the superintendent, or, in his absence, from the chief magistrate in attendance on the spot; or, in their absence, from a member of the fire-engine committee, and from no other person whatever.

V.--FIREMEN.

The firemen shall attend at all times when required by the head enginemen or superintendent, as well as upon the days of general inspection. They shall keep their engines in good order and condition, and shall be equipped in their uniform at all times when called out.

They shall observe the instructions of no person whatever, except those of the superintendent or head enginemen.

VI.--HIGH CONSTABLES AND COMMISSIONERS OF POLICE.

Upon occasions of fire, the moderator of the high constables shall call out the high constables, and, if necessary, he shall also call out the extra constables, and give notice to call out the constables of their districts; and it shall be the duty of the constables to preserve order and to protect property, to keep the crowd away from the engines, and those employed about them; and, when authorized by the chief magistrate, superintendent of engines, or, in the absence of a magistrate, by a member of the committee on fire-engines, to provide men for working the engines.

Neither the constables nor the commissioners of police shall assume any management, or give any directions whatsoever, except in absence of a magistrate and the superintendent of engines, in which case any member of the committee on fire-engines may give orders to the head enginemen.

In cases of protracted fire, when extra men may be required to relieve the regular establishment, it shall be the duty of the high constables to collect those wanted, from amongst the persons on the street who may be willing to lend their assistance, mustering them in such parties as may be required, taking a note of their names, and furnishing each individual with a certificate or ticket, with which the moderator of the high constables, or chief constable at the time, will be supplied; and no person shall receive any remuneration for alleged assistance given at a fire who may not produce such certificate or ticket.

The party or parties so mustered shall be placed and continue under the care of two high constables, until required for service, when they shall be moved forward to the engine.

The men relieved by the party so moved forward, shall be taken charge of by two high constables, who shall see them properly refreshed and brought back within a reasonable time, so that the men employed may thus occasionally relieve each other without confusion, and without being too much exhausted.

VII.--MAGISTRATES, &c.

Upon occasion of fires, the magistrates, sheriff, moderator of the high constables, the superintendent of the water company, the managers of the different gas-light companies, and the fire-engine committee, will give their attendance. They will assemble in such house nearest to the place of the fire as can be procured, of which notice shall be immediately given to the officer commanding the police on the spot.

The orders of the chief magistrate in attendance shall be immediately obeyed; and no order, except those issued by such magistrate, and the particular directions given as to the fire and engine department by the master of engines, or, in their absence, by a member of the fire-engine committee on the spot, shall be at all attended to.

The magistrates and sheriff further declare, that all porters holding badges shall be bound to give their attendance at fires when called upon for that purpose.

VIII.--GAS-LIGHT COMPANIES.

The managers of the different gas-light companies, on receiving notice of a fire, shall instantly take measures for turning off the gas from all shops and houses in the immediate neighbourhood of the fire.

IX.--SPECIAL REGULATIONS FOR THE FIREMEN.

Captains.--On the alarm of fire being given, an engine must be immediately despatched from the main office to whatever district the fire may be in; and the captain in whose district the fire happens shall bring his engine to the spot as quickly as possible, taking care that none of the apparatus is awanting. On arriving at the spot, he must take every means in his power to supply his engine with water, but especially by a service-pipe from a fire-cock, if that be found practicable. Great care must be taken to place the engine so that it may be in the direction of the water, with sufficient room on all sides to work it, but as little in the way of persons employed in carrying out furniture, &c., as possible. He must also examine the fire while the men are fixing the hose, &c., that the water may be directed with the best effect.

The captains shall be responsible for any misconduct of their men, when they fail to report such misconduct to the superintendent.

The engines must be at all times in good working order, and the captain shall report to the superintendent when any part of the apparatus is in need of repair.

When the fire is in another district, the captain of each engine shall get his men and engine ready to proceed at a moment's notice, but must not move from his engine-house till a special order arrives from a lieutenant of police or the superintendent of brigade.

Sergeants.--The sergeant of each engine will take the command in absence of the captain. When the captain is present, the sergeant will give him all possible assistance in conducting the engine to the fire; and it will there be more particularly the sergeant's duty to see that the engine is supplied with water, and that every man is at his proper station, and to remain with his engine while on duty, whether it is working or not, unless he receives special orders to the contrary.

Pioneers.--Nos. 1, 2, 3, and 4 of each engine will be considered pioneers. Nos. 1 and 2 will proceed to the fire immediately, without going to their engine-house, in order to prepare for the arrival of the first engine, by ascertaining and clearing a proper station for it, and by making ready the most available supplies of water, as also to examine the state of the premises on fire and the neighbouring ones, so as to be able to give such information to the captain on his arrival as may enable him to apply his force with the greatest effect. The pioneers will attend particularly to the excluding of air from the parts on fire by every means in their power, and they will ascertain whether there are any communications with the adjoining house by the roof, gable, or otherwise. When the several engines arrive, the pioneers will fall in with their own company, and take their farther orders from the captain or sergeant.

Firemen.--On the alarm of fire being given, the whole company belonging to each engine (Nos. 1 and 2 excepted) shall assemble as speedily as possible at their engine-house, and act with spirit under the orders of their officers in getting everything ready for service. Each man will get a ticket with his own number and the colour of his engine marked upon it; and on all occasions when he comes on duty he will give this ticket into the hands of a policeman, who will be appointed by the officer of police on duty to collect them at each engine-house, and who will accompany the engine if it is ordered to the fire.

If the ticket be not given in, as before provided, within half an hour after the alarm is given at their engine-house, or at all events, within half an hour after the arrival of the engine at the fire, the defaulter will forfeit the allowance for turning out, and also the first hour's pay.

If not given in within the first hour, he will forfeit all claim to pay.

The superintendent, however, may do away the forfeiture in any of these cases, on cause being shown to his satisfaction.

On quarter-days and days of exercise, every man must be ready equipped at the appointed hour, otherwise he will forfeit that day's pay, or such part of it as the superintendent may determine.

Any man destroying his equipments, or wearing them when off duty, will be punished by fine or dismissal from the service, as the superintendent may determine.

Careless conduct, irregular attendance at exercise, or disobedience of superior officers, to be punished as above-mentioned.

The man who arrives first at the engine-house to which he belongs, properly equipped, will receive three shillings over and above the pay for turning out.

The first of the Nos. 1 and 2 who arrives at the fire, properly equipped, in whatever district it may be, will receive three shillings over and above the pay for turning out.

No pay will be allowed for a false alarm, unless the same is given by a policeman.

As nothing is so hurtful to the efficiency of an establishment for extinguishing fires as unnecessary noise, irregularity, or insubordination, it is enjoined on all to observe quietness and regularity, to execute readily whatever orders they may receive from their officers, and to do nothing without orders.

The first engine and company which arrive at the fire are not to be interfered with, nor their supplies of water diverted from them by those coming afterwards, unless by a distinct order from the superintendent, or, in his absence, from the chief magistrate on the spot. The same rule will apply to each succeeding engine which takes up a station.

The men must be careful not to allow their attention to be distracted from their duty by listening to directions from any persons except their own officers; and they will refer every one who applies to them for aid to the superintendent, or to the chief magistrate present at the time.

All the firemen must be particularly careful to let the policemen on their respective stations know where they live, and take notice when the policeman is changed, that they may give the new one the requisite information.

The men are particularly cautioned not to take spirituous liquors from any individual without the special permission of the captain of their engine, who will see that every proper and necessary refreshment be afforded to them; and as intoxication upon such alarming occasions is not merely disreputable to the corps, but in the highest degree dangerous, by rendering the men unfit for their duty, every appearance of it will be most rigidly marked; and any man who may be discovered in that state shall not only forfeit his whole allowances for the turn-out and duty performed, but will be forthwith dismissed from the corps.

All concerned are strictly enjoined to preserve their presence of mind, not to lose temper, and upon no occasion whatsoever to give offence to the inhabitants by making use of uncivil language or behaving rudely.

*** Every one belonging to the establishment will be furnished with a printed copy of these Regulations, which they are enjoined carefully to preserve and read over at least once every week.

MEANS OF ESCAPE FROM FIRE.

[The following was written in the year 1830, and does not refer to Public Fire-Escapes other than those that can be carried with a Fire-Engine.--EDITOR.]

When the lower floors of a house are on fire, and the stairs or other ordinary means of retreat destroyed, the simplest and easiest mode of removing the inhabitants from the upper floors, is by a ladder placed against the wall. In order to be able at all times to carry this plan into effect, the person having charge of the engines should (as far as possible) inform himself where long ladders are to be had, and how they can most easily be removed.

But if a ladder of sufficient length is not to be procured, or is at too great a distance to render it safe to wait for it, recourse must immediately be had to other means.

If it happens that the windows above are all inaccessible, on account of the flames bursting through those below, the firemen should immediately get on the roof (by means of the adjoining houses,) and descend by the hatch. The hatch, however, being sometimes directly above the stair, is in that case very soon affected by the fire and smoke. If, on approaching, it is found to be so much so as to render an entrance in that way impracticable, the firemen should instantly break through the roof, and, descending into the upper floors, extricate those within. If it should happen, however, that the persons in danger are not in the upper floor, and cannot reach it in consequence of the stair being on fire, the firemen should continue breaking through floor after floor till they reach them. In so desperate a case as this the shorter process may probably be to break through the party-wall between the house on fire and that adjoining, when there is one; and when there is no house immediately contiguous, through the gable, taking care in either case to break through at the back of a closet, press, chimney, or other recess, where the wall is thinnest. If an opening has been made from the adjoining house, it should immediately (after having served the purpose for which it was made) be built up with brick or stone, to prevent the fire spreading. All these operations should be performed by slaters, masons, or house-carpenters, who, being better acquainted with such work, are likely to execute it in a shorter time than others--time, in such a case, being everything, as a few minutes lost may cost the lives of the whole party. It is not impossible, however, that circumstances may occur to render all or either of these plans impracticable; in that case, one or two of the lower windows must be darkened, and by this means access gained to the upper ones. The plan recommended by the Parisian firemen is, for a man to wrap himself up in a wet blanket, and thus pass swiftly through the flames. But this effort is only to be attempted when the flames from a single door are to be passed; in any other case the stair will most likely be in flames, and impassable.

A simple means of escape from fire is to have an iron ring fastened to the window sill, and inside of the room a cradle, with a coil of rope attached to it. The rope is put through the ring, and the person wishing to escape gets into the cradle, and lowers himself down by passing the rope through his hands. The great objection to this plan, which is certainly very simple, is the difficulty, or rather impossibility, of persuading people to provide themselves with the necessary materials. Many men, too, are incapable of the exertion upon which the whole plan depends; and if men in a state of terror are unfit for such a task, what is to become of women and children?

Any fire-escape, to be generally useful, must, in the first place, be capable of being carried about without encumbering the fire-engine; and, in the next place, must be of instant and simple application. The means which appear to me to possess these qualifications in the highest degree, is a combination of the cradle plan, with Captain Manby's admirable invention for saving shipwrecked seamen.

The apparatus necessary for this fire-escape is a chain-ladder eighty feet long, a single chain or rope of the same length as the ladder, a canvas bag, a strong steel cross-bow, and a fine cord of the very best workmanship and materials, 130 feet long, with a lead bullet of three-ounce weight attached to one end, and carefully wound upon a wooden cone seven inches high and seven inches broad at the base, turned with a spiral groove, to prevent the cord slipping when wound upon it, also a small pulley with a claw attached to it, and a cord reeved through it of sufficient strength to bear the weight of the ladder.

In order to prevent the sides of the ladder from collapsing, the steps are made of copper or iron tube, fastened by a piece of cord passed through the tube and into the links of the chain, till the tube is filled. The steps thus fastened are tied to the chain with copper-wire, so that, in the event of the cord being destroyed, the steps will be retained in their places by the wire. The ladder is provided with two large hooks at one end, for the purpose of fixing it to a roof, window-sill, &c. The bag is of canvas, three feet wide and four feet deep, with cords sewed round the bottom, and meeting at the top, where they are turned over an iron thimble at each side of the mouth of the bag. The steel cross-bow is of the ordinary description, of sufficient strength to throw the lead bullet with the cord attached, 120 feet high.

When the house from which the persons in danger are to be extricated is so situated that the firemen can get to the roof by passing along the tops of the adjoining houses, they will carry up the chain-ladder with them, and drop it over the window where the inmates show themselves, fastening the hooks at the same time securely in the roof. The firemen will descend by the ladder into the window, and putting the persons to be removed into the bag, lower them down into the street by the single chain. If the flames are issuing from the windows below, the bag, when filled, is easily drawn aside into the window of the adjoining house, by means of a guy or guide-rope.

If the house on fire stands by itself, or if access cannot be had to the roof by means of the adjoining houses, the lead bullet, with the cord attached, is thrown over the house by means of the cross-bow; to this cord a stronger one is attached, and drawn over the house by means of the former; a single chain is then attached, and drawn over in like manner; and to this last is attached the chain-ladder, which, on being raised to the roof, the firemen ascend, and proceed as before directed.

If the house be so high that the cord cannot be thrown over far enough to be taken hold of by those on the opposite side, then the persons to be extricated must take hold of the cord, as it hangs past the window at which they may have placed themselves. By means of it they draw up the small pulley, and hook it on the window-sill. The chain-ladder is then made fast to the end of the cord, and drawn up by those below. When the end of the chain-ladder comes in front of the window, the persons inside fasten the hooks of the ladder on its sill, or to the post of a bed, the bars of a grate, or anything likely to afford a sufficient hold. After having ascertained that the ladder is properly fixed, the firemen will ascend and proceed as in the former cases.

I must here remark, that before this plan can be properly put in execution, the firemen must be regularly trained to the exercise. When the firemen here are practised with the fire-escape, the man ascending or descending has a strong belt round his middle, to which another chain is fastened, and held by a man stationed at the window for that purpose; if any accident, therefore, were to occur with the chain-ladder, the man cannot fall to the ground, but would be swung by the chain attached to the belt round his body. The men are also frequently practised in ascending and descending by single chains. The firemen here are very fond of the above exercise; the bagging each other seems to amuse them exceedingly.[I]

The last resort, in desperate cases, is to leap from the window. When this is to be attempted, mattresses, beds, straw, or other soft substances, should be collected under the window; a piece of carpet or other strong cloth should be held up by ten or twelve stout men. The person in the window may then leap, as nearly as possible, into the centre of the cloth, and if he has sufficient resolution to take a fair leap, he may escape with comparatively little injury.[J]

FIRE-ENGINES.

In the application of manual power to the working of fire-engines, the principal object is, to apply the greatest aggregate power to the lightest and smallest machine; that is, suppose two engines of the same size and weight, the one with space for 20 men to work throws 60 gallons per minute; and the other, with space for 30 men, throws 80 gallons in the same time; the latter will be the most useful engine, although each man is not able to do so much work as at the former.

The reciprocating motion is generally preferred to the rotary for fire-engines. Independent of its being the most advantageous movement, a greater number of men can be employed at an engine of the same size and weight; there is less liability to accident with people unacquainted with the work, and such as are quite ignorant of either mode of working, work more freely at the reciprocating than the rotary motion. To these reasons may be added, the greater simplicity of the machinery.

Various sizes of engines, of different degrees of strength and weight, have been tried, and it is found that a fire-engine with two cylinders of 7 inches diameter, and a stroke of 8 inches, can be made sufficiently strong at 17-1/2 cwt. If 4 cwt. be added for the hose and tools, it will be found quite as heavy as two fast horses can manage, for a distance under six miles, with five firemen and a driver.

This size of engine has been adopted by the Board of Admiralty and the Board of Ordnance, and its use is becoming very general.

When engines are made larger, it is seldom that the proper proportions are preserved, and they are generally worked with difficulty, and soon fatigue the men at the levers.

When an engine is large, it not only requires a considerable number of men to work it, but it is not easily supplied with water; and, above all, it cannot be moved about with that celerity on which, in a fire-engine establishment, everything depends. When the engine is brought into actual operation, the effect to be produced depends less on the quantity of water thrown than upon its being made actually to strike the burning materials, the force with which it does so, and the steadiness with which the engine is worked. If the water be steadily directed upon the burning materials, the effect even of a small quantity is astonishing.

When a large engine is required in London, two with 7-inches cylinders are worked together by means of a connecting screw, thus making a jet very nearly equal (as 98 to 100) to that of an engine with cylinders 10 inches diameter.

It is also an advantage not unworthy of consideration, that two 7-inch engines may be had nearly for the price of one 10-inch one; so that if one happens to be rendered unserviceable the other may still be available.

The usual rate of working an engine of the size described is 40 strokes of each cylinder per minute; this gives 88 gallons. The number of men required to keep steadily at work for three or four hours is 26; upwards of 30 men are sometimes put on when a great length of hose is necessary. The lever is in the proportion of 4-1/4 to 1. With 40 feet of leather hose and a 7/8 inch jet, the pressure is 30 lb. on the square inch; this gives 10.4 lbs. to each man to move a distance of 226 feet in one minute. The friction increases the labour 2-1/2 per cent. for every additional 40 feet of hose, which shows the necessity of having the engine, and of course the supply of water, as close to the fire as is consistent with the safety of the men at the levers.

In order that the reader may have a distinct idea of such a fire-engine, I shall here endeavour to give a description, chiefly taken from those made by W. J. Tilley,[K] fire-engine maker, London.

The engravings (figs. 1 and 2) represent a fire-engine of 7-inch barrels and 8-inch stroke.[L] The cistern marked A is made of mahogany or oak. The upper work, B, and side-boxes or pockets, C, are of Baltic fir. The sole, D, upon which the barrels stand, and which also contains the valves, is of cast-iron, with covers of the same material, which are screwed down, and the joints made good with leather or india-rubber. The pieces E, at each end of the cast-iron sole D, are of cast brass, and screwed to the cast-iron sole D, with a joint the same as above. In one of these pieces is the screwed suction-cap F, and to the other is attached the air-vessel G, made of sheet-copper, and attached to the piece E by a screw. The exit-pipe H is attached to the under side of the casting E by a swivel. The valves at I are of brass, ground so as to be completely water-tight. The barrels K are of cast brass. The engine is set on four grasshopper springs M. The shafts or handles O, of the levers P, are of lancewood. The box S, under the driving seat, is used for keeping wrenches, cord, &c.; in the fore part of the cistern A, and the box B above the cistern, the hose is kept; the branch and suction-pipes are carried in the side-boxes or pockets C; the rest of the tools and materials are kept along with the above-mentioned articles, in such situations as not to interfere with the working of the engine.

The cistern is made of oak or mahogany, for strength and durability; but, for the sake of lightness, the upper work and side-boxes are made of Baltic fir, strength in them being of less importance.

As the valve cannot be made without a rise for the lid to strike against, there is a small step at each of the valves, and the sole is carried through as high as this step, to admit of the water running off when the engine is done working. If constructed in a different manner, the water will lodge in the bottom, and produce much inconvenience in situations where the engine is exposed to frost.

The valve-covers are of cast-iron, fastened down with copper screws, a piece of leather or india-rubber being placed between them and the upper edges of the sole.

The pieces at each end of the sole are of cast-brass, instead of sheet-copper, with soft-solder joints, which are very apt to give way.

The screwed suction cap with iron handle admits the water in two different directions, according as it is open or closed: the one to supply the engine when water is drawn from the cistern, the other for drawing water through the suction-pipe.

The valves are brass plates, truly ground to fit the circular brass orifice on which they fall. The brass being well ground, no leather is used for the purpose of making them tight. The longer they are used the better they fit, and by having no leather about them they are less liable to the adhesion of small stones or gravel. The whole valve is put together and then keyed into a groove in the sides and bottom of the sole, left for that purpose.

The barrels are of cast-brass, with a piston made of two circular pieces of the same metal, each put into a strong leather cup, and bolted to the other. The bottoms of the cups being together, when the piston becomes loose in the barrels, and there is not sufficient time to replace the cups by new ones, they are easily tightened by putting a layer of hemp round the piston between the leather and the brass. This operation, however, requires to be carefully performed; for if more hemp is put into one part than another it is apt to injure the barrels. The barrels are fixed to the cast-iron sole by copper screws, a little red lead being placed between the bottom flange of the barrel and the sole.

When the engine is likely to be dragged over rough roads or causeways, it is of importance to have it set on springs, to prevent the jolting from affecting the working part of the engine, everything depending on that being right.

The engines used in Paris are mounted on two wheels, the carriage and the engine being separate, the latter being dismounted from the former before it can be used. In Paris, where the engines are managed by a corps of regularly-trained firemen, this may answer well enough; but if hastily or carelessly dismounted by unskilful persons, the engine may be seriously damaged. It is also worthy of remark, that the proper quantity of hose, tools, &c., can be more easily attached to and carried on a four-wheeled engine.

In order that the men may work more easily at the handles, and suffer less fatigue, the engine is not higher than to enable them to have the levers easily under their command. The shafts of the levers are of lancewood, being best calculated to bear the strain to which they are exposed when the engine is at work, and they are made to fold up at each end for convenience in travelling.

The air-vessel should be placed clear of any other part of the engine, excepting only the point where it is attached.

The fore-carriage of the engine is fitted with a pole, and is made to suit the harness of coach-horses, these being, in large towns, more easily procured than other draught cattle; this can be altered, however, to suit such harness as can most readily be obtained. Where horses are seldom used to move the engines, a drag-handle is attached, by which one or two men are able easily to direct the progress of the engine.

Two drag-ropes, each twenty-five feet long, of three-inch rope, with ten loops to each, are attached, one to each end of the splinter-bar, by means of which the engines are dragged; and to prevent the loops collapsing on the hand, they are partly lined with sheet-copper.

The whole of the brass work of an engine should be of the best gun-metal, composed of copper and tin only. Yellow brass should never be used; even at first it is far inferior to gun-metal, and after being used for some time it gets brittle. The whole of the materials used in the construction of a fire-engine should be of the best description.

In London for some years past a hand-pump has been carried with each engine. They have been found of the greatest service in keeping doors, windows, &c., cool. They throw from six to eight gallons per minute, to a height of from thirty to forty feet, and can be used in any position. The idea of the hand-pumps I took from the old-fashioned squirt, or "hand-engine."

When fire-engines are unserviceable it arises more frequently from want of care in keeping in order than from any damage they may have received in actual service or by the wearing out of the materials; so it is quite plain that this important part of the duty has not generally had that degree of attention paid to it which it deserves.

Although an engine were to be absolutely perfect in its construction, if carelessly thrown aside after being brought home from a fire, and allowed to remain in that state till the next occasion, it would be in vain (especially in small towns, where alarms are rare) to expect to find it in a serviceable condition; some of the parts must have grown stiff, and if brought into action in this state something is likely to give way.

When an engine is brought back from a fire, it ought to be immediately washed, the cistern cleaned out, the barrels and journals cleaned and fresh oil put on them, the wheels greased, and every part of the engine carefully cleaned and examined, and if any repairs are needed they should be executed immediately. When all this has been attended to clean hose should be put in, and the engine is again fit for immediate service. Besides this cleaning and examination after use, the engine ought to be examined and the brass part cleaned once a week, and worked with water once a month whether it has been used or not.

In addition to the keeping of the engine always in an effective state, this attention has the advantage of reminding the men of their duty, and making them familiar with every part of the mechanism of the engine; thus teaching them effectually how the engines ought to be protected when at work, by enabling them to discover those parts most liable to be damaged, and to which part damage is the most dangerous. It is more troublesome generally to get the engines well kept when there are no fires, than when there are many. But the only effectual method of inducing the men to keep them in good order, in addition to the moral stimulants of censure and applause, is to fine those who have the charge of them for the slightest neglect.

When the engine has been properly placed, before beginning to work the fore-carriage should be locked. This is done by putting an iron pin through a piece of wood attached to the cistern, into the fore-carriage. This prevents the wheels from turning round, and coming under the shafts, by which the latter might be damaged, and the hands of the men at work injured.

Small stones, gravel, and other obstructions, sometimes find their way into the nozzle of the branch-pipe, from having dropped into the hose before being attached, or having been drawn through the suction-pipe or from the cistern. Whenever the engine is found to work stiffly, it should be stopped and examined, otherwise the pressure may burst the hose, or damage some part of the engine. If anything impedes the action of the valves the pistons must be drawn, and if a person's hand be then introduced they may easily be cleared--constant care and attention to all the minuti?of the engine and apparatus being absolutely indispensable, if effective service be expected from them.

Considerable attention ought to be paid to the selecting a proper situation for an engine-house. Generally speaking, it ought to be central, and on the highest ground of the district it is meant to protect, and care should be taken to observe when any of the streets leading from it are impassable.

If, in addition to these advantages, the engine-house can be had adjoining to a police watch-house, it may be considered nearly perfect, in so far as regards situation. These advantages being all attained, the engine can be conveyed to any particular spot by a comparatively small number of men, while the vicinity of a police watch-house affords a facility of communicating the alarm of fire to the firemen not to be obtained otherwise. When the engine-house is placed in a low situation the men who first arrive must wait till the others come forward to assist them to drag the engine up the ascent, and many minutes must thus be lost at a time when moments are important.

After choosing a proper situation for the engine-house, the next care should be directed towards having it properly ventilated, as nothing contributes more to the proper keeping of the engines and hose than fresh and dry air. For this purpose a stove should be fitted up, by which the temperature may be kept equal. When engines are exposed to violent alternations of heat and cold, they will be found to operate very considerably on the account for repairs, besides occasioning the danger of the engine being frozen and unserviceable when wanted.

There ought to be at least half a dozen keys for each engine-house, which should be kept by the firemen, watchmen, and those connected with the establishment, that the necessity of breaking open the door may not occur.

DESCRIPTION OF TOOLS WITH WHICH EACH ENGINE IS PROVIDED.

Having considered the sort of fire-engine which is best adapted for general purposes, I shall now notice the different articles which, in London, are always attached to, and accompany, each engine of this kind:--

7 coils of hose, 40 feet each. 4 bundles of sheepskin and lay-cord. 4 lengths of suction-pipe, each between 6 and 7 feet long. 2 branch pipes. 3 jet pipes or nozzles and an elbow for jet. 3 wrenches for coupling-joints. 2 lamps. 2

lengths of scaling ladder. 1 fire-hook. 60 feet of patent line, and 20 feet of trace line. 1 mattock. 1 shovel. 1 hatchet or pole-axe. 1 saw. 1 iron crow-bar. 1 portable cistern. 1 flat suction strainer. 1 standcock, and hook for street plugs. 1 screw wrench. 1 canvas sheet with 10 or 12 rope handles round its edges. 9 canvas buckets. 1 hand-pump with 10 feet of hose and jet pipe.

Of these articles I shall endeavour to give a description as they stand in the above list.

The article of hose being first in order, as well as importance, merits particular attention.

The sort used is leather, made with copper rivets, and is by far the most serviceable and durable hose that I have yet seen.

Manufacturers of this article, however, for a very obvious reason, are not always careful to select that part of the hide which, being firmest, is best adapted for the purpose. Indeed, I have known several instances wherein nearly the whole hide has been cut up and made into hose, without any selection whatever. The effect of this is very prejudicial. The loose parts of the hide soon stretch and weaken, and while, by stretching, the diameter of the pipe is increased, the pressure of the water, in consequence, becomes greater on that than on any other part of the hose, which is thereby rendered more liable to give way at such places.

Hose are frequently made narrow in the middle, and, in order to fit the coupling-joints, wide at the extremities--a practice which lessens their capability of conveying a given quantity of water, in proportion to the difference of the area of the section of the diameters at the extremity and the middle part.

In order to make them fit the coupling-joints, when carelessly widened too much, I have frequently seen them stuffed up with brown paper, and in that case they almost invariably give way, the folds of the paper destroying the hold which the leather would otherwise have of the ridges made on the ends of the coupling-joints.

In order to avoid all these faults and defects, the riveted hose used are made in the following manner:--

The leather is nine and five-eighths inches broad (that being the breadth required for coupling-joints of two and a half inches diameter of clear water-way), and levelled to the proper uniform thickness. The leather used is taken from hides of the very best description, perfectly free from flesh-cuts, warble-holes, or any other blemish, and stuffed as high as possible.[M] Not more than four breadths are taken from each hide, and none of the soft parts about the neck, shoulders, or belly are used. No piece of leather is less than four feet long.

The leather is gauged to the exact breadth, and holes punched in it for the rivets. In the operation of punching, great care must be taken to make the holes on each side of the leather exactly opposite to each other. If this precaution be not attended to, the seam when riveted takes a spiral direction on the hose, which the heads of the rivets are very apt to cut at the folds. Care must also be taken that the leather is equally stretched on both sides, otherwise the number of holes on the opposite sides may be unequal. The ends are then cut at an angle of thirty-seven degrees; if cut at a greater angle, the cross-joint will be too short, and if at a smaller, the leather will be wasted. This must, however, be regulated in some degree by the number of holes in the cross-joint, as the angle must be altered a little if the holes at that part do not fit exactly with the holes along the side.

The different pieces of leather necessary to form one length, or forty feet of hose, are riveted together by the ends.

Straps of leather, three inches broad, are then riveted across the pipe, ten feet apart, to form loops for the purpose of handing or making fast the hose when full of water. The leather is then laid along a bench, and a bar of iron, from eight to ten feet long, three inches broad, and one inch thick, with the corners rounded off, is laid above it. The rivets are next put into the holes on one side of the leather, along the whole length of the iron bar. The holes on the other side are then brought over them, and the washers put on the points of the rivets, and struck down with a hollow punch. The points of the rivets are then riveted down over the washers, and finished with a setting punch. The bar of iron is drawn along, and the same operation repeated till the length of the hose be finished.

The rivets and washers should be made of the best wrought copper, and must be well tinned before being used.

Some objections have been made to riveted hose on account of the alleged difficulty of repairing them; but this is not so serious a matter as may at first view appear. Indeed, they very seldom require any repairs, and when they do, the process is not difficult. If any of the rivets be damaged, as many must be taken out as will make room for the free admission of the hand. A small flat mandrel being introduced into the hose, the new rivets are put into the leather, and riveted up the same as new pipe; the mandrel is then shaken out at the end.

If the leather be damaged, it may be repaired either by cutting out the piece, and making a new joint, or by riveting a piece of leather upon the hole.

The manner of attaching the hose to the coupling-joint is also a matter of very considerable importance. If a joint come off when the engine is in operation, a whole length of hose is rendered useless for the time, and a considerable delay incurred in getting it detached, and another substituted.

To prevent this, the hose ought to fit as tightly as possible to the coupling-joint, without any packing. In riveted hose, a piece of leather, thinned down to the proper size, should be put on to make up the void which the thick edge of the leather next the rivet necessarily leaves; the hose should then be tied to the coupling-joint as firmly as possible with the best annealed copper wire, No. 16 gauge.

When the hose are completely finished in this manner they are proved by a proving-pump, and if they stand a pressure of two hundred feet of water they are considered fit for service. I may also add, that when any piece of hose has been under repair it is proved in the same manner before it is deemed trustworthy.

The proving of the hose is of very considerable importance, and the method of doing so which I have mentioned is greatly superior to the old plan of proving them on an engine or fire-cock. By the latter method, no certain measure can be obtained by which the pressure can be calculated. In the first place it must depend on the relative height of the reservoir from whence the water is obtained and that of the fire-cock where the experiment is made; and as the supply of water drawn from the pipes by the inhabitants may be different on different days of the week and even in different hours of the day, it is quite evident that by this method no certain rule can be formed for the purpose required, the pressure being affected by the quantity of water drawn at the time.

The method of proving by an engine is considerably better than this; but when a proving-pump can be obtained it is infinitely better than either. One disadvantage of an engine is, that it requires a considerable number of men; but even the proof, that of throwing the water to a given height on the gable of a house or other height, is not always a test of the sufficiency of the hose. As the temperature is low or high, the wind fresh or light, the degree of pressure on the hose in throwing the water to the required height will be greater or less. Indeed, in high winds it is a matter of extreme difficulty to throw the water to any considerable height.

With an engine of 7-inch barrels and 7-inch stroke, fitted with eighty feet of 2-3/8-inch hose, I have found from several experiments that when the water is thrown seventy-five feet high, the pressure on the hose is equal to one hundred feet. The same engine, with 160 feet of hose, and the branch-pipe raised fifty feet above the level of the engine, when the water was thrown fifty-six feet from the branch, occasioned a pressure equal to 130 feet on the hose. From these experiments, I am convinced that the pressure will not be equal to 200 feet, except in very extreme cases, or when some obstacle gets into the jet pipe.

I tried the extreme strength of a piece of riveted hose 4 feet long and 2-3/8 inches diameter, and found that it did not burst till the pressure increased to 500 feet; and when it gave way the leather was fairly torn along the rivet-holes.

Every possible care should be taken to keep the hose soft and pliable, and to prevent its being affected by mildew. After being used, in order to dry them equally they should be hung up by the centre, with the two ends hanging down, until half dry. They should then be taken down and rubbed over with a composition of bees'-wax, tallow, and neats-foot oil,[N] and again hung up to allow the grease to sink into the leather. When the hose appear to be dry they should be a second time rubbed with the composition, and then coiled up for use. In order that the hose undergoing the operation of greasing may not be disturbed or used till in a fit state, it is better to have a double set, and in this way, while one set is in grease the other is in the engine ready and fit for service. More time can also be taken for any repairs which may be necessary, and they will in consequence be more carefully done, and at fires where a great length of hose is required the spare set will always be available. When the weather is damp, and the hose cannot be dried so as to be fit for greasing in two or three days, a stove should be put into the room in order to facilitate the process. The greatest care, however, must be taken in the use of artificial heat. The whole apartment should be kept of one equal temperature, which ought never to be higher than is requisite to dry the hose for greasing in about forty hours.

Coupling-joints.[O]--So much of the efficiency and duration of the hose depend on the proper form given to the brass coupling-joints, that I deem it useful to give a detailed description, both of those generally made use of and of those adopted by the Edinburgh fire-establishment, and also to point out their various defects and advantages.

Fig. 3 is the construction commonly made by engine-makers. Its defects are as follows:--From the form of the furrows and ridges where the leather is tied it does not hold on well against a force tending to pull the hose off end-ways; screw-nails are therefore often employed, as at A, to secure the hose on the brass. The points of these nails always protrude more or less into the inside of the joint, and materially impede the current of water. The mouths of the joints are also turned outwards, and form a shoulder, as at B. The intention of this is probably to assist in securing the leather in its place, and to prevent the lapping from slipping. The effects of it are as follows:--First, from the leather being strained over this projection, it becomes liable to be cut by every accidental injury, and very soon cracks and gives way, when a portion must be cut off and a fresh fixing made; second, the leather being stretched over the projection, does not fit the other part of the joint, and must be loose or filled up with pieces of leather, or, as is sometimes done, with brown paper; third, the irregularity of the calibre of the conduit which this shoulder occasions diminishes the performance of the engine.

Fig. 4 is the coupling-joint adopted in Edinburgh. The furrows at the tying place are shallow, but their edges present a powerful obstacle to the slipping of the leather. No screw-nails are employed, nor is there any shoulder, as at B; there is therefore no impediment to or variation in the velocity of the current, as the calibres of the coupling joints and of the hose are so nearly uniform. It will be seen also that as the lapping projects above the leather this latter can never be injured by falls or rubbing on the ground.

Another great advantage attending the joints used here is the manner in which their screws are finished. On examining the figure minutely, it will be observed that the male-screw ends in a cylinder of the diameter of the bottom of its thread, consequently of the diameter of the top of the thread of the female-screw. The effect of this is, that, when the screws are brought together, the cylindric portion serves as a guide to the threads, and the most inexperienced person cannot fail to make them catch fair at the first trial. The advantage of this in the circumstances attending fires is obvious.

These joints, although requiring three or four turns to close them up, yet as it is only the ring D which requires to be turned, it can easily be done with the hand alone without the use of wrenches. Although, when the whole length of hose has been jointed, it may be as well to send a man with a pair of wrenches to set the joints firm; this, however, is by no means absolutely necessary; if the joints are kept in proper order a man can secure them sufficiently with the hand.

There is also a facility in taking turns out of the hose, which no other but a swivel joint affords. By slackening a single turn any twist may be taken out, without undoing the joint or stopping the engine, while, from the number of turns required to close the joints, there is no chance of the screw being by any accident undone. In order to prevent the threads from being easily damaged, they should be of a pretty large size, not more than five or six to the inch. For the same reason also the thread should be a little rounded.

As it sometimes happens that the screws are damaged by falling on the street, or by heavy bodies striking them, whenever the hose have been used the joints should be tried by a steel gauge-screw, to be kept for that purpose. This ought to be particularly attended to, as, on arriving at a fire, it is rather an awkward time to discover that a joint has been damaged, while the delay thus occasioned may be attended with very serious consequences.

Four Bundles of Sheepskin and Lay-cord.--These are simply four or five stripes of sheepskin, each about three or four inches broad. When a leak occurs in a length of hose which cannot be easily replaced at the time, one or more pieces of sheepskin are wrapt tightly over the leak and tied firmly with a piece of cord. This is but an indifferent method of mending, but I do not know of any other which can be so readily applied with the same effect. If another length of hose can be substituted for the leaky one it is better to do so; but that is not always at hand, nor does it always happen that time can be spared for the purpose.

Four Lengths of Suction-pipe.--These are generally made of leather, riveted tightly over a spiral worm of hoop-iron, about three-quarters of an inch broad, a piece of tarred canvas being placed between the worm and the leather. They are usually made from six to eight feet long, with a copper strainer screwed on the farther end, to prevent as much as possible any mud or dirt from getting into the engine with the water. It is of advantage to carry four lengths of suction-pipe, as they can be joined to reach the water; if one is damaged the others will still be serviceable.

The suction-pipes are more troublesome to rivet than the common hose, and are done in the following manner:--After the joints are fixed on the spiral worm, and it is covered with the tarred canvas, an iron mandrel longer than the worm is put through it, the edge being rounded to the circle of the inside of the worm. The projecting ends of the mandrel are supported to allow the worm to lie quite clear. One end of the mandrel has a check, that the brass joint may not prevent the worm from lying flat on the mandrel. The leather is then put over the worm, and the rivets being put into one side, a small thin mandrel is laid over the canvas and the rivets struck down upon it. If the small mandrel be not used the heads of the rivets are apt to lie unequally on the worm.

Three Wrenches for Coupling-joints.--These are for tightening the coupling-joints, when that cannot be sufficiently done by hand. When the hose are all put together a man is sent along the whole line with a pair of wrenches to tighten such of the coupling-joints as require it. The wrenches are generally made with a hole to fit the knob on the coupling-joint, and, when used, are placed, one on the nob of the male and another on the nob of the female-screw, so as to pull them in opposite directions.

Two Branch Pipes.--These are taper copper tubes, having a female-screw at one end to fit the coupling-joints of the hose, and a male-screw at the other to receive the jet pipes, one is 4 feet long to use from the outside of a house on fire, the other 12 inches for inside work.

Three Jet-pipes or nozzles of various sizes made to screw on the end of the branch pipe.

A great many different shapes of jet have been tried, and that shown in Fig. 5, I found to answer best when tried with other forms. The old jet was a continuation in a straight line of the taper of the branch, from the size of the hose-screw, to the end of the jet-pipe; this had many inconveniences; the size of the jet could not be increased without making the jet-pipe nearly parallel. As the branches were sometimes 7 feet or 8 feet long, in some instances the orifice at the end of the jet-pipe was larger than that at the end of the branch. The present form of the jet completely obviates this difficulty, as the end of the branch is always 1-1/2 inches diameter.

The curve of the nozzle of the present jet is determined by its own size; five times one-half of the difference between the jet to be made and the end of the branch, is set up on each side of the diameter of the upper end of the branch, a straight line is then drawn across, and an arc of a circle described on this line, from the extremity of each end of the diameter of the jet, until it meets the top of the branch; the jet is then continued parallel, the length of its own diameter; the metal is continued one-eighth of an inch above this, to allow of a hollow being turned out to protect the edge: The rule for determining the size of the jet for inside work is, to "make the diameter of the jet one-eighth of an inch for every inch in the diameter of the cylinder, for each 8 inches of stroke." The branch used in this case is the same size as shown in Fig. 5. When it is necessary to throw the water to a greater height, or distance, a jet one-seventh less in area is used, with a branch from 4 feet to 5 feet long.

Two Lengths of Scaling Ladders.--These are 6-1/2 feet long, and are fitted with sockets so that any number up to 7 or 8 may be joined together to form one ladder varying in length according to circumstances from 6-1/2 to upwards of 40 feet.

One Fire-hook.--This is similar to a common boat-hook, of such length as may be most convenient to strap on the handles of the engine. It is used for pulling down ceilings, and taking out deafening-boards when the fire happens to be between the ceiling and the floor above. It is also used when a strong door is to be broken open. It is placed with the point upon the door, one or two men bearing upon it, while another striking the door, the whole force of the blows is made to fall upon the lock or other fastening, which generally yields without much difficulty.

Sixty Feet of Patent Line and Twenty Feet of Trace Line.--These are generally used for hoisting the hose into the windows of the house, in which there is a fire, the stairs being sometimes so crowded with people and furniture, that it is difficult to force a passage, and when the pipe is laid in the stair, it is liable to be damaged by people treading on it.

One Mattock and Shovel.--These are useful in damming any running water or gutter, uncovering drains, &c., from which the engine may be supplied with water. The mattock should be short and strong, and the shovel of the sort called diamond-pointed.

One Hatchet.--The most serviceable hatchet for a fire-engine, is similar to that used as a felling axe by wood-cutters. The back part is made large that it may be conveniently used as a hammer.

One Saw.--This should be a stout cross-cut saw, very widely set. It is useful in cutting off the communication between one house and another, which, when water is scarce, is sometimes necessary.

One Iron Crow-bar.--This should be about two feet long. It is used in opening doors, breaking through walls, &c.

One Portable Cistern.[P]--This is made of canvas on a folding iron frame, and is used in London placed over the street-fire plugs, a hole is left in the bottom through which the water enters and fills the cistern, the escape between the canvas and the plug box being trifling. Two and sometimes three engines are worked by suction-pipe from one plug in this manner. The portable cistern is also used when the engine is supplied by suction, from water conveyed in carts or buckets, and is greatly preferable to any plan of emptying the water directly into the engine. By this latter method there is always a considerable waste of water, arising both from the height of the engine, and the working of the handles; and, in addition to these objections only one person can pour in water at a time. When the water is poured into the engine from carts, it must stop working till the cart is emptied. All these objections, are in a great measure removed by placing the portable cistern clear of the engine; when used in this manner there must of course be no hole in the bottom.

One Flat Suction Strainer, made to screw on to the suction pipe, to prevent anything being drawn in that would not pass through the jet-pipe, and made flat, with no holes in the upper surface, for use in the portable cistern.

One Standcock, with stem to insert direct in the fire-plug, and used principally with hose to throw a jet for cooling ruins.

One Canvas Sheet.--This, when stretched out and held securely by several men, may be jumped into from the window of a house on fire with comparative safety.

One Hand-pump, as described at page 130, and used with the canvas buckets.

FOOTNOTES:

[Footnote G: The engines and their crews are distinguished by these colours.]

[Footnote H: The hose are made up in flat coils, with the male coupling-screw in the centre, and the female on the outside. When a length is to be laid out in any direction, it is set on its edge, and then run out in the required direction,--in this way no turns or twists can ever occur. When the hose is to be taken up, it is uncoupled, and then wound up, beginning at the end farthest from the engine or from the fire-cock (as the case may be): by this method all the water is pressed out.]

[Footnote I: In practising this exercise the men are in the habit of descending by the chains from the parapet of the North Bridge, Edinburgh, to the ground below: a height of 75 feet.]

[Footnote J: Mr. Braidwood used canvas jumping sheets on this principle with hand holes for a dozen men, in the ordinary service of the London Fire Brigade.]

[Footnote K: Now Shand, Mason, and Co.]

[Footnote L: This description applies to the most recently constructed fire-engines belonging to the Metropolitan Fire Brigade.]

[Footnote M: "Stuffing," a technical term need by leather-dressers or curriers.]

[Footnote N: The proportions are, 1 gallon neats-foot oil, 2 lbs. tallow, 1/4 lb. bees-wax, melted together, and laid while warm on the leather.]

[Footnote O: This description of the Edinburgh coupling-joints was written in 1830, and is inserted here to show how the present form of the well-known London Brigade hose-coupling was arrived at. The internal diameter was originally 2-3/8 inches, but Mr. Braidwood, when in London, found that he could increase it to 2-1/2 inches.]

FIRE ANNIHILATOR

With regard to the Fire Annihilator, I have seen several experiments with this machine, and heard of more which were not successful; and if an invention fails when experiments are tried, it is open to the impression that it might fail when brought into active operation. There have also been many cases where these machines have met with accidents, one at Drury Lane Theatre amongst the number.

Water, properly applied, will do whatever the Annihilator can accomplish, and also many things which the latter cannot do. As it is, there are some forty or fifty different articles to carry with each fire-engine, and to add to them such unwieldy things as Fire Annihilators, would be to encumber the men more than they are at present, with a very doubtful prospect of advantage.

WATER SUPPLY.

The supply of water is the most vital part of any exertions towards extinguishing fire. Where the pressure is sufficient, and the mains large enough, by far the most efficient and economical mode of using the water is to attach the hose directly to the mains.

In London, however, this can rarely be done, for several reasons. The greatest number of plugs are on the service pipes, that is, the pipes for supplying water for domestic and other purposes, which are only open a short time every day. If the cisterns are nearly empty, the pressure cannot be obtained till they are filled. Then, again, the plugs being some distance apart, it is difficult to obtain a sufficient number of jets. But when the plugs are full open 1-3/4 diameter, a sufficient quantity of water is obtained from each to supply three engines, each of which will give a jet equal to the plug if confined to one jet. The pressure also in the mains in London seldom exceeds 120 feet at the utmost. For these reasons the pressure from the mains is seldom used till the fire is checked, when the ruins are cooled by the "dummies," as the jets from the mains are named by the firemen.

If water can be obtained at an elevation, pipes with plugs or firecocks on them, are preferable to any other mode at present in use for the supply of fire-engines. The size of the pipes will depend on the distance and elevation of the head, and also on the size of the buildings to be protected. It may be assumed as a general rule, that the intensity of a fire depends, in a great measure, on the cubic content of the building; distinction being made as to the nature and contents of such building. If no natural elevation of water can be made available, and the premises are of much value, it may be found advisable to erect elevated tanks; where this is done, the quantity of water to be kept ready, and the rate at which it is delivered, must depend on the means possessed of making use of the water.

The average size of fire-engines may be taken at two cylinders of 7 inches diameter, with a length of stroke of 8 inches, making forty strokes each per minute. This sized engine will throw 141 tons of water in six hours, and allowing one-fourth for waste, 176 tons would be a fair provision in the tanks for six hours' work; this quantity multiplied by the number of engines within reach, will give an idea of what is likely to be required at a large fire. If, however, there are steam-engines to keep up the supply through the mains, the quantity of water kept in readiness may be reduced to two hours' consumption, as it is likely that the steam-engines would be at work before that quantity was exhausted. This is what may be supposed to be required, in cases of serious fires in dockyards, in large stacks of warehouses, or in large manufactories.

Where water can be had at nearly the level of the premises, such as from rivers, canals, &c., if it is not thought prudent to erect elevated tanks, the water may be conducted under the surface by large cast-iron pipes, with openings at such distances as may seem advisable for introducing the suction-pipes (Fig. 6). This plan should not be adopted where the level of the water is more than 12 feet below the surface of the ground, as although a fire-engine will, if perfectly tight, draw from a much greater depth than 14 feet (2 feet being allowed for the height of the engine), still a very trifling leakage will render it useless for the time, at such a depth.

The worst mode of supplying engines with water is by covered sunk tanks; they are generally too small, and unless very numerous, confine the engines to one or two particular spots, obliging the firemen to increase the length of the hose which materially diminishes the effect of the fire-engine. If the tank is supplied by mains from a reservoir, it would be much better to save the expense of the tank, and to place plugs or firecocks on the water-pipe. Another evil in sunk tanks is, that the firemen can seldom guess what quantity of water they may depend upon, and they may thus be induced to attempt to stop a fire, at a point they would not have thought of if they had known correctly the quantity of water in store.

Where sunk tanks are already constructed, they may be rendered more available by a partial use of the method shown in Fig. 6.

Memoranda of Experiments tried on the mains and service pipes of the Southwark Water Company, between 4 and 9 A.M. of the 31st January, 1844. The wind blowing fresh from N.N.W.

The pressure at the water-works at Battersea was kept at 120 feet during the experiments, and every service pipe or other outlet was kept shut.

1st Experiment.--Six standcocks, with one length of 2-1/2 inches riveted leather hose 40 feet long, and one copper branch 4 feet to 5 feet long, with a jet 7/8 inch in diameter on each, were placed in six plugs on a main 7 inches diameter, in Union-street, between High-Street, Borough, and Gravel-lane, Southwark, at distances of about 120 yards apart. The water was brought from the head at Battersea, by 4250 yards of iron pipes 20 inches diameter, 550 yards of 15 inches diameter, and 500 yards of 9 inches diameter.

1st. One standcock was opened, which gave a jet of 50 feet in height, and delivered 100 gallons per minute.

With four lengths of hose the jet was 40 feet high, and the delivery 92 gallons per minute. When the branch and jet were taken off with one length of hose the delivery was 260 gallons per minute.

2nd. The second standcock was then opened, and the jet from the first was 45 feet high.

3rd. The third standcock was opened, and the jet from the first 40 feet high.

4th. The fourth standcock being opened, the first gave a jet of 35 feet high.

5th. The fifth being opened, the first gave a jet of 30 feet high.

6th. All the six being opened, the first gave a jet of 27 feet in height.

2nd Experiment.--Six standcocks were then put into plugs, on a main 9 inches diameter in Tooley-Street, the extreme distance being 450 yards, with hose and jets as in the first experiment. The water was brought from the head at Battersea by 4250 yards of iron pipes of 20 inches diameter, 1000 yards of 15 inches diameter, 1400 yards of 9 inches diameter. The weather was nearly the same, but the place of experiment was more protected from the wind than in Union-street.

1st. With one standcock open, a jet 60 feet in height was produced, and 107 gallons per minute were delivered.

2nd. The second standcock was then opened, and the difference in the first jet was barely perceptible.

3rd. Other two standcocks being opened, the first jet was reduced to 45 feet in height, and the delivery to 92 gallons per minute.

4th. All the six standcocks being opened, the first jet was further reduced to 40 feet high, and the delivery to 76 gallons per minute.

3rd Experiment.--Two standcocks, with hose, &c., as in the first experiment, were then put into a service-pipe, 4 inches diameter and 200 yards long, in Tooley-street, the service-pipe was connected with 200 yards of main 5 inches diameter, branching from the main of 9 inches diameter. The weather was still the same as at first, but the wind did not appear to affect the jets, owing to the buildings all round being so much higher than the jet.

1st. The standcock nearest the larger main was opened, and a jet of 40 feet high was produced, delivering 82 gallons per minute.

2nd. Both standcocks being opened, the first gave a jet of 31 feet, and delivered 68 gallons per minute.

3rd. The standcock farthest from the large main only being opened, gave a jet of 34 feet, and delivered 74 gallons per minute.

4th. Both standcocks being opened, the farthest one gave a jet of 23 feet, and delivered 58 gallons per minute.

When both these plugs were allowed to flow freely without hose, the water from that nearest the large main, rose about 18 inches, and the farther one about 1 inch above the plug-box.

These and other experiments prove the necessity of placing the plugs on the mains, and not on the service pipes, where there are mains in the street.

The different modes of obtaining water from the mains or pipes are shown in the accompanying drawings.

(Fig. 8) is a section of the common plug, with a canvas dam or cistern over it, as used in London. The cistern is made of No. 1 canvas, 15 inches deep, extended at top and bottom by 5/8-inch round iron frames, a double stay is hinged on the top frame at each end. When the cistern is used the top frame is lifted up, and the stays put into the notches, in two pieces of hoop iron, fixed to the bottom frame. There is a circular opening 9 inches diameter in the canvas bottom, two circular rings of wash-leather, about 2 inches broad, are attached to the edges of the opening in the canvas, so as to contract it to 4 inches or 5 inches diameter; the plug being opened, the cistern is placed over it; the wash-leather is pressed down to the surface of the road by the water, and a tolerably water-tight cistern, with about 12 inches or 14 inches of water in it, is immediately obtained.

It will be observed, that the short piece of pipe between the main and this firecock is not curved to the current of the water, but merely opened a little; this is done with a view of increasing the supply by steam power, and as the steam engines are, in most cases, situated in a different direction from the tanks or reservoirs, therefore the curve that would have assisted the current in one direction would have retarded it in the other. It has been objected to these firecocks, that the opening does not run through the centre of the key, therefore only one side of the key covers the opening in the barrel, while in the common firecock both sides are covered.

This has a very good delivery, and is certain to be always tight, if well made, as the pressure of the water forces the key into the barrel; this also renders the cock somewhat difficult to be opened and shut, if the pressure be great; but as a lever of any length may be used, and the key, from its perpendicular position, may be loosened by a blow, this objection is in a great measure obviated.

In Figs. 10 and 11 the openings in the street are large enough to admit of the levers for opening the cock to be fixed, that no mistake may occur from the lever being mislaid; but with those at the British Museum, it was not thought necessary to have fixed levers, as a crow-bar, or anything that could be introduced into the eye of the spanner, would open them.

The plug and firecock have both certain advantages and disadvantages, which are now described.

The plug, with a canvas cistern, is the easiest mode of obtaining water; the plug-box being only the size of a paving-stone, is no annoyance in the street, and the water has only one angle to turn before it is delivered.

On the other hand, where the supply of water is limited, the plugs give but little command of it; there is, however, comparatively very small loss at a large fire in London from this cause, as it is very seldom that all the fire-engines can be supplied direct from the plugs, and those that arrive late must pick up the waste water as they best can, by using another description of canvas dam, or opening the street; but in enclosed premises, especially where the water is kept for the purpose of extinguishing fires, firecocks are much to be preferred. It is very difficult to insert the standcock into a plug if there is a considerable force of water, and if the paving has moved, it cannot be done without raising the plug-box; but this is, however, the easiest mode of using firecocks, and where there is a considerable pressure of water, if the watchmen or the police are supplied with a hose-reel and branch-pipe, they can, in enclosed premises, direct a jet on the fire while the engines are being prepared, and if they cannot reach the fire, they will have water ready for the engine when it arrives.

Inclosed premises are particularly mentioned, because the principal duty of the watchmen, in these cases, is to guard against fire, and their other duties being comparatively few, the men are not often changed, and they can be instructed thoroughly in the matter. With the general police of the metropolis it is quite different, their duties are so numerous and varied, that to add that of firemen to them would only be to confuse them.

Firecocks, if kept at 9 inches to 12 inches below the surface, are easily protected from frost, by stuffing the opening with straw.

The advantage which the double firecocks have over the single ones, is merely the increased water-way, as a firecock 3-1/2 inches diameter could not be so easily opened or shut, as two cocks of 2-1/2 inches diameter.

One of the greatest objections to firecocks, is the very large openings required in the streets, the first cost and the repair of which are both considerable, besides their liability to accident. To take them to the footpath, increases the expenses and diminishes the supply of water, as it is generally done with a small pipe, and the number of angles is increased. In some instances, where firecocks have been put down on one side of the street, no less than four right angles have been made in the course of the water; and if the fire happens to be on the opposite side of the street from the firecock, the thoroughfare must be stopped. The expense also is no slight consideration, for if laid along with the water-pipes, each firecock, if properly laid, and the pit built round with cement, will cost eight or ten times as much as a plug.

London is, upon the whole (except in the warehouse districts), fairly supplied with water for the average description of fires, that is, where not more than five or six engines are required. When, however, it is necessary to work ten or twelve engines, there is very often a deficiency. In many of the warehouse districts the supply is very limited indeed, although it is there that the largest fires take place.

The water companies are generally willing to give any quantity of water, but they object to lay down large mains without any prospect of remuneration. The warehouse keepers decline to be at the expense of laying the pipes, and there the matter seems to rest. In most other places of importance, the water is under the management of the civic authorities, and they, of course, endeavour to obtain a good supply of water at fires in warehouse as well as in other districts.

In supplying fire-engines with water from firecocks, one or more lengths of hose are screwed on the firecock; the extreme end being put into the engine, the firecock is then opened and the water rushes in. When the water-pipes are large and the pressure considerable, two or even three engines may be supplied from the same firecock.

If the firecocks are all at too great a distance from the place on fire, to be reached by the supply of hose brought with the engine, the next resource is, to open the nearest firecock above the level of the place where the water is required. By covering the eyes of drains, and stopping up any cross-water channels, the water may in this manner be conveyed along the street, from a very considerable distance. From the nature of the ground it does not always happen that the water will run directly from the nearest firecock, to the spot where it is required; acclivities, buildings, and many other causes, may prevent this; but in some of these cases a few lengths of the hose, attached to the firecock, may convey the water to a channel which will conduct it to the required point. Upon the arrival of the water, it ought to be dammed up, and the engine will lift it by suction out of the pool so formed.

If, however, from the nature of the ground, from the want of hose, or from other causes, it is found impracticable to convey the water by either of the above methods, the next best is, to conduct the water in hose as far as can be accomplished, and carry it the remainder of the distance in carts, buckets, or whatever else may be most convenient.

When carried in buckets it is of advantage to form a line of men from the water to the engine, each man covering five or six feet of ground. The buckets are then handed from one man to another, till they reach the two or three men who are stationed round the suction-tub or fire-engine to receive them. The buckets when emptied are returned by a different line of men (women or boys) stationed in the same manner as the former. If a sufficient number of hands cannot be had to return the buckets in this manner, any convenient number may be employed to carry them to the firecock, that they may be again filled. When a fire occurs where the water-pipes are unprovided with firecocks or plugs, the ground should be immediately opened, and the water-pipe cut. If it be of cast-iron, a large hammer may effect the purpose: on the water-pipe being broken, the suction-pipe of the engine is placed in the opening so made. If the pipe be of lead, the opening in the street should be made of sufficient length to admit of one end of it, when cut, being turned into the engine. If the supply of water by this means be so great as to occasion waste, it may be regulated by the nearest stopcock on the water-pipe, by driving a wooden plug into the end of a cast-iron pipe, or compressing the end of a leaden one.

The next plan I shall notice of supplying fire-engines is from drains, gutters, &c. In particular situations and wet weather considerable supplies of water from these and similar sources may be obtained. In the gutters all that is required is to dam them up; and, if there be no materials at hand for this purpose, the causeway must be dug up, till there is a sufficient depth of water for the suction-pipe of the engine.

When the water is to be drawn from drains or common sewers, great care should be taken not to damage them farther than is absolutely necessary.

If enough of cover be taken off to allow one man to enter easily, it will be quite sufficient for all necessary purposes. When the man inside the drain or common sewer has collected a proper supply of water by damming up the channel, the suction-pipe should be handed down to him, and the engine set to work.

Although it be true that foul water quenches fire, I will here observe, that the water from a common sewer should never be used, except when it is impossible to procure it from a purer source. For the purpose of procuring water to extinguish a fire, I had at one time occasion to open a common sewer, in which, with the usual impurities, the waste from a gas manufactory was intermixed, and the stench in the premises where the fire had been extinguished by this water, was for some time after very disagreeable.

If the water be obtained from a pond or river at a little distance, one engine may be stationed close to it, and that engine made to pump the water into another at work. If the water be conveyed in carts, an engine may be kept at the pond or river for the purpose of filling them. Of course this can only be done where there is a proper supply of engines.

In working from an open water, such as a gutter, drain, river, or pond, it is proper, in order to prevent sand or gravel being drawn into the engine, to sink an iron or wooden bucket, into which the suction-pipe of the engine should be placed. If nothing better can be had, a good wicker basket will be found useful.

It is of great advantage to have a number of carts, with butts upon them full of water, as it ensures a small supply to the engines the moment they arrive at the fire. This plan, however, entails a very considerable expense, as carters must be paid for taking them out on every alarm, besides giving prizes to the owners of the first and second horses, to ensure their coming in time.

APPENDIX.

The following, on Steam Fire-engines and the Metropolitan Fire Brigade, is added as a supplement to Mr. Braidwood's account of the London Fire Brigade, and brings the information upon these subjects up to the present date (May, 1866):--

The steam fire-engine was first constructed in London, in 1830, before the formation of the London Fire Brigade, by Braithwaite, who made several engines, and exhibited them at various public trials, also at several fires, but without being able to bring them into general use.

The matter remained in abeyance till 1852, when the London Fire Brigade caused their large hand-worked floating fire-engine to be altered so as to be worked by steam. This engine having been originally made by Tilley, of London, the alterations were entrusted to Shand and Mason, his successors. In the same year the first American steam fire-engine was constructed in New York.

In 1855 the London Fire Brigade, stimulated by their first experiment, caused an entirely new self-propelling, floating steam fire-engine to be constructed. The experience gained by their first attempt at steam fire-engine making, enabled Shand and Mason to compete successfully in this matter, as their design was adopted after receiving the approval of the late Mr. Walker, Engineer, of Great George Street, London.

The re-introduction of land steam fire-engines into London was accomplished by Shand and Mason, who, in 1858, constructed their first; this engine, after several public trials, was in the same year sent to St. Petersburgh.

In 1859 the same firm constructed two land steam fire-engines, which they offered to the London Fire Brigade for hire or purchase, and in the following year (1860) the Fire Brigade took one on hire for one year. This experiment proved so successful, that in 1861 the committee purchased, from Shand and Mason, the fourth steam engine of their construction. This, with one of the two made in 1859, were the only land steam engines that were at work at the Great Tooley Street Fire of 1861.

In the beginning of 1862, Mr. Lee, of the firm of Lee and Larned, of New York, brought over a land steam fire-engine to be placed in the International Exhibition. This was worked in public at Hodges' Distillery on the 24th of March previous to the opening of the Exhibition.

Shand and Mason supplied the London Fire Brigade in April, 1862, with the eighth land steam fire-engine of their construction. Messrs. Merryweather and Sons, of London, placed their first land steam fire-engine in the International Exhibition of 1862, but this, like the ninth by Shand and Mason, was not in time for the opening, and consequently could not compete for a prize medal, which was awarded to Lee and Larned, of New York.

A public trial, however, took place before the jury of the Exhibition, of which the following is an account extracted verbatim from the jurors' published reports:--

INTERNATIONAL EXHIBITION, 1862.

SPECIAL JURY FOR FIRE-ENGINES.

J. F. BATEMAN, F.R.S., London; Civil Engineer.

CAPT. BENT, London; Superintendent of Fire Arrangements in the Exhibition.

W. M. BROWN, London; Superintendent of Westminster Fire Brigade.

EARL OF CAITHNESS, London.

J. HAWKSHAW, London; Civil Engineer.

C. JENNY, Austria; Councillor of Mines in the Imperial Royal Academy of Mines at Schemnitz.

P. LUUYT, France; Engineer to the Imperial Commissioners of Mines.

J. E. McCONNELL, Wolverton; late Locomotive Superintendent of the London and North Western Railway.

O. PIHL, Norway; Civil Engineer.

W. M. RANKINE, Glasgow; Professor of Mechanics in the University of Glasgow.

CAPT. SHAW, London; Superintendent of the London Fire Brigade.

DUKE OF SUTHERLAND, London.

F. B. TAYLOR, United States; Mechanical Engineer.

H. THOMAS, Zollverein; Manufacturer.

H. TRESCA, France; Professor of Mechanics, President of the French Institute of Civil Engineers.

REPORT OF THE SPECIAL COMMITTEE OF CLASS VIII. ON FIRE-ENGINES.

After detailing the Trials of Hand-worked Fire-Engines, the Report states that,--

The Committee next proceeded to take the necessary steps for trying the steam fire-engines on the 1st of July, and, as before, invited the engine builders to a preliminary meeting, that they might receive full information as to the rules and regulations to be observed.

In compliance with this invitation, the following engine-makers attended a meeting on the 28th of June, viz:--

Mr. Lee, of the firm of Lee and Larned, Novelty Iron-works, New York.

Messrs. Merryweather and Son.

Messrs. Shand and Mason.

Mr. Lee declined to produce his steam fire-engine for trial, alleging various reasons for so doing, and though strongly urged, persisted in his resolution, and declined the contest.

Messrs. Merryweather and Son expressed themselves ready to produce their steam fire-engine on the appointed day.

Messrs. Shand and Mason informed the Committee that the engine which they had intended to work would not be ready owing to an accident, but requested permission to produce for trial two steam-engines made by them for the London Fire-Engine Establishment, although they were not in the Exhibition. All the arrangements having been made for trying several engines together, the Committee granted this request, as otherwise only one engine would have been present, and a complete table of results could therefore not have been obtained.

The Committee assembled in the appointed place at eight o'clock on the morning of the 1st of July, and found three engines present, viz., one of Messrs. Merryweather and Son and two of Messrs. Shand and Mason.

After the Committee had examined the boilers and machinery generally, the engine-makers filled their respective boilers with cold water from the river, and fires having been laid, the three were lighted at the same moment, and the makers were ordered to commence working into a tank at sixty feet distance as soon as they had attained a steam pressure of 100 lbs. to the square inch.

Messrs. Merryweather's engine attained the pressure named in 12 minutes 10 seconds, Messrs. Shand and Mason's large engine in 18 minutes 30 seconds, the small engine in about 30 minutes, some mismanagement having occurred which compelled them to draw the fire in the latter and light it a second time. Messrs. Merryweather's engine commenced working as arranged when the steam-gauge indicated a pressure of 100 lbs., and was 2 minutes and 50 seconds at work before water passed through the nose-pipe. Notwithstanding this very serious defect, this engine had poured 500 gallons of water into a tank 60 feet distant in 17 minutes and 15 seconds from the time at which the fire was lighted. After the difficulty of drawing the water had been surmounted, this engine worked well, and threw an admirable jet, losing 15 lbs. steam-pressure during the first trial. After three trials this engine became disabled; it was, however, repaired on the ground in about an hour and a half, and resumed work at the ninth trial, continuing to work well until the thirteenth, when it became again disabled, and was withdrawn by the maker, to the great regret of the Committee, who were thus left to continue the experiments with only two engines, both made by one firm.

Messrs. Shand and Mason's large engine was 18 minutes 30 seconds getting up steam to 100 lbs., and when started drew water instantly, losing during the first trial 5 lbs. of steam-pressure.

This engine was severely tested, and worked without accident throughout the day, the seventeenth trial lasting no less than 63 minutes, during which the steam and water were both kept to a pressure of 90 lbs. on the square inch throughout, working through a 1-3/8 inch nose-pipe.

At the eighteenth and last trial this engine threw a good vertical jet.

Messrs. Shand and Mason's small engine did not raise the steam to 100 lbs. in less than 30 minutes, owing, of course, partly to the mismanagement already mentioned, and partly to the nature of the boiler and fire-box, which, according to the makers' account, are not adapted for raising steam in the shortest possible time. After the engine got to work the steam-pressure was well sustained, and the engine continued working the entire day without accident, concluding in the evening by throwing a good vertical jet.

During the time occupied by the trials the direction of the wind was W.N.W. to W. by N., pressure 2-1/2 to 4-1/2 lbs. on the square foot. The barometer stood at 29.97 inches.

Summary.

On the whole the Committee find as follows:--

Messrs. Merryweather and Son have produced, at a price of 700l., a steam fire-engine, weighing, according to the makers' account, 65 cwt., with jets and lamps, but without water, coal, suction-pipes, hose, or other gear, and capable, if no accidents occur, of throwing in an available stream the following average quantities of water per minute:--

Distance. Angle. Quantity.

61 feet. 10?230 gallons. 85 " 21?124 "

Messrs. Shand and Mason have produced an engine, at a cost of 650l., weighing, according to their statement, 55 cwt., with jets and lamps, but without water, coals, suction-pipes, hose, or other gear, and capable of throwing in an available stream the following average quantities of water per minute:--

Distance. Angle. Quantity.

61 feet. 10?250 gallons. 63 " 18?165 " 82 " 14?172 " 85 " 21?137 " 102 " 11?94 " 104 " 17?19 "

Messrs. Shand and Mason have also produced, at a price of 370l., an engine which, under the same conditions, weighs 35 cwt., and is capable of throwing in an available stream the following average quantities per minute:--

Distance. Angle. Quantity.

61 feet. 10?142 gallons. 63 " 18?133 " 82 " 14?56 " 85 " 21?27 "

The best performance during the five trials from which this last average was taken being forty-six gallons, and the lowest five gallons per minute.

At greater distances, in consequence of the wind, this engine could not deliver a stream, but continued working without accident throughout the day, and concluded in the evening by throwing a good vertical jet.

SUTHERLAND, CHAIRMAN. E. M. SHAW, HON. SEC.

* * * * *

Shand and Mason's tenth land steam fire-engine was supplied to the London Brigade in June, 1862, and their twelfth, in February, 1863, upon orders given on the 4th January, 1862. But as the Committee of the London Fire Brigade were now negotiating with Government to take the duty of extinguishing fires off their hands, no orders for steam-engines were given out by them after the above date.

* * * * *

STEAM FIRE-ENGINE COMPETITION,

CRYSTAL PALACE, LONDON, 1863.

Towards the close of 1862, several engineers and other gentlemen interested in the improvement of steam fire-engines, offered prizes to be awarded at competitive trials to take place in London. The following is the Committee's published account of these trials which were held in the grounds of the Crystal Palace Company on the 1st, 2nd, and 3rd July, 1863.

The Committee consisted of the following gentlemen, viz.:--

Chairman.

HIS GRACE THE DUKE OF SUTHERLAND.

Members.

THE RIGHT HON. THE EARL OF CAITHNESS. LORD RICHARD GROSVENOR, M.P. J. G. APPOLD, ESQ. J. T. BATEMAN, ESQ. W. M'BROWNE, ESQ. T. R. CRAMPTON, ESQ. W. M. CROSSLAND, ESQ. W. FAIRBAIRN, ESQ. T. HAWKSLEY, ESQ. J. E. McCONNELL, ESQ. HENRY MAUDSLAY, ESQ. J. MATHEWS, ESQ. J. NASMYTH, ESQ. J. PENN, ESQ. WILLIAM SMITH, ESQ.

Hon. Sec.

CAPTAIN E. M. SHAW.

The engines were divided into two classes, the large class consisting of those weighing over 30 cwts., and not exceeding 60 cwts. and the small class of those not exceeding 30 cwts.

The prizes offered were 250l. for the best engine, and 100l. for the second best, in each class.

The chief points to which the Committee directed their attention, in addition to the consideration of cost and weight, were those relating to the general efficiency of the machines as fire-engines, combining among other points of excellence--

Rapidity in raising and generating steam.

Facility of drawing water.

Volume thrown.

Distance to which it can be projected with the least amount of loss.

Simplicity, accessibility, and durability of parts.

LARGE CLASS.

FIRST TRIAL.

Delivering 1000 gallons into a tank at a true distance of 67 feet, and 27?from the horizon. Depth from which water was drawn, 4 feet 6 inches. The water in the boiler being cold when the signal was given to commence, each engine commencing to work on attaining steam pressure of 100lb. to the square inch.

No.	MAKER.	Weight.	Time of raising Steam to 100lbs.	Time of filling Tank.	Total
		T. c. q. lbs.	' "	' "	' "
1	Easton & Amos, London	2 18 3 12	13 14	6 16	19 30
2	Merryweather & Son, London	2 18 0 8	10 25	9 42	20 7
3	Shand & Mason, London	2 17 1 0	10 51	12 19	23 10
4	Butt and Co., United States	2 14 0 4	16 30	6 48	23 18
5	Roberts, London	1 19 1 4	11 40	20 24	32 4
	Nichols (Manhattan) United States	2 10 1 4	Did not work.		
	Gray & Son, London	1 18 1 4	Did not work.		

MERRYWEATHER AND SON began to work at 100 lbs., fell directly to 40 lbs., and continued so throughout; stopped and steam rose to 130 lbs.

SHAND AND MASON--Suction-pipe choked; left off working about 2 minutes.

SECOND TRIAL.

Delivering 1000 gallons into tank at same distance commencing with full steam.

+-----+--------------------+------------+--------+---------+ | | | Steam at | Steam |
Time of | | No. | NAME. | Beginning. | during | filling | | | | | Work. | Tank. |
+-----+--------------------+------------+--------+---------+ | | | | | ' " | | 1 | Shand &
Mason | 100 | | 3 0 | | | | | | | | 2 | Butt & Co. | 100 | | 3 3 | | | | | | | | 3 |
Merryweather & Son | 145 | | 3 7 | | | | | | | | 4 | Roberts | 80 | | 12 30 | +-
----+--------------------+------------+--------+---------+ Roberts did not fill the tank.

THIRD TRIAL.

Delivering into large tank at a horizontal distance of 40 feet, a vertical height of 40 feet, a true distance of 56 feet, and at an angle of 45 degrees from the horizon, the depth from which water was drawn being 16 feet 4 inches.

Key: A--No. of Deliveries Open. B--Length of Hose. C--Average Steam Pressure. D--Average Water Pressure. E--No. of Gallons Delivered.

+-----+-----------+---------+---+---+--------+----+----+-------+-------+ | | | | | |Size of
| | | |Time of| |No.| Name. | Time. | A | B |Nozzle. | C | D | E |Raising| | |
| | | | | | | |Steam. | +---+-------------+---------+---+---+--------+----+----+-------+---
----+ | | |hr. m. s.| | | | | | | | 1 | Merryweather| 1 24 55 | 2 |440| 1-1/2 |
91 | 89 |16,086 |10' 32"| | | & Son | | | | | | | | to | | | | | | | | | | | | |
80lbs.| | | | | | | | | | | | 2 | Shand | 2 0 0 | 2 |440| 1-1/2 &| 96 | 62
|12,917 |11' 21"| | | & Mason | | | | 1-3/8 | | | | to | | | | | | | | | | |
|120lbs.| | | | | | | | | | | | | 3 | Roberts | 2 0 0 | 1 |420| 1-1/4 | 75 | 75 |
9,936 |11' 20"| | | | | | | | | | | to | | | | | | | | | | | 80lbs.| | | | | | | | | | |
| | | 4 | Butt & Co. | 0 46 50 | 2 |440| 1-1/2 | 78 | 78 | 8,280 |14' 10"| | | |
| | | | | | | to | | | | | | | | | | | | 45lbs.| | | | | | | | | | | | | 5 | Easton & | 1
32 35 | 2 |440| 1-3/8 | 98 | 41 | 3,036 |12' 30"| | | & Amos | | | | | | | | to

```
| | | | | | | | | | 90lbs.| | | | | | | | | | | | 6 | Nichols | 0 4 55 | 2 |420|
1-1/2 | -- | -- | None. |13' 09"| | | (Manhattan) | | | | | | | | to | | | | | | | |
| | | 45lbs.| +---+-------------+---------+---+---+--------+----+----+-------+-------+
```

MERRYWEATHER AND SON--Fire lighted at 4h. 1m. 55s.; gauge moved at 4h. 8m. 20s.; engine started at 4h. 12m. 27s.; water drawn in about 10 revolutions; pumps not primed, valve box leaked slightly, and engine worked satisfactorily in every respect.

SHAND AND MASON--Fire lighted at 11h. 25m. 46s.; gauge moved at 11h. 32m. 53s.; engine started at 11h. 37m. 7s.; pump primed at 11h. 45m. 48s.; drew water at 11h. 47m.; water first through the nozzle at 11h. 48m. 59s.; in hood at 11h. 49m. 19s.; shifted nozzle (3-1/4m. delay); high wind.

ROBERTS--Fire lighted at 11h. 17m.; engine, started at 11h. 28m. 20s.

BUTT AND CO.--Fire lighted at 5h. 55m. 10s.; started engine at 6h. 9m. 20s.; repeatedly stopped from slide valves not acting, and stopped entirely at 6h. 46m., from cylinder cover breaking.

EASTON AND AMOS--Fire lighted at 2h. 2m. 35s.; gauge moved 2h. 10m.; started engine at 2h. 15m. 5s.; pumps primed, worked till 2h. 54m. 5s.; stopped to shift plungers; went to work again, and stopped entirely at 3h. 35m. 10s., from two fire bars falling out.

NICHOLS (Manhattan)--Fire lighted at 10h. 51m. 14s.; gauge moved at 10h. 59m. 20s.; drew water directly; steam up to 140lbs. at 11h. 8m. 45s.; stopped two minutes; started again; made a few revolutions, and fly-wheel broke.

FOURTH TRIAL

Vertical Jet against Tower.

```
+-----+--------------------+---------+-----------------+ | No. | Name. | Size | Greatest
Height | | | | of Jet. | Thrown. | +-----+--------------------+---------+-----------------+
| 1 | Shand & Mason | 22/16 | 180 ft. | | | | | | | 2 | Merryweather & Son |
26/16 | 180 ft. | | | | | | | 3 | Roberts | 14/16 | 150 ft. | | | | | | | 4 | Lee &
Co | 21/16 | 55 ft. | +-----+--------------------+---------+-----------------+
```

GRAY'S engine lighted fire at 7h. 7m. 40s.; steam 9lbs. at 7h. 17m. 0s.; got to work at 7h. 23m. 40s. to blow fires; at 7h. 27m. 0s. water through hose. Owing to some of the pipe connected with the steam gauge breaking, no further experiments could be made.

SMALL CLASS.

FIRST TRIAL.

Delivering 1000 gallons into a tank at a true distance of 50ft. and 37?from the horizon. Depth from which water was drawn, 4ft. 6in. The water in the boilers being cold when the signal was given to commence, each engine commencing to work on attaining steam pressure of 100lbs. to the square inch.

No.	Name.	Weight.	Time of raising to 100lbs.	Time of filling	Total Time.	Time of Steam	Time of Tank.
		T. c. q. lbs.	' "	' "	' "		
1	Shand & Mason	1 9 2 0	11 36	5 24	17 0		
2	Lee & Co	1 10 0 0	11 55	6 3	17 58		
3	Merryweather & Son	1 10 1 12	12 15	9 14	21 29		

Owing to a broken bolt, there was great leakage in water cylinder of Lee and Co's. engine.

SECOND TRIAL.

Delivering 1000 gallons into tank at same distance, commencing with full steam.

No.	Name.	Steam at Beginning.	Steam during Work.	Time filling Tank.
				' "
1	Shand & Mason	85	--	5 49
2	Lee & Co.	125	--	5 50
3	Merryweather & Son	100	--	6 17

The leakage in Lee and Co's. engine was remedied.

THIRD TRIAL.

Delivering into large tank, commencing with Full Steam. At a horizontal distance of 40ft., a vertical height of 40ft., a true distance of 56ft., and at an angle of 45?from the horizon; the depth from which water was drawn being 16ft. 4in.

Key A--Number of Deliveries open. B--Average Steam Pressure. C--Average Water Pressure. D--No. of Gallons Delivered.

Name.	No.	Time. h. m. s.	A	Length of Hose.	Size of Nozzle. in.	B	C	D
Shand & Mason	1	1 0 0	1	420	1 & 1-1/4	146	80	8142
Merryweather & Son	2	1 0 0	1	420	7/8	86	45	4885
Lee & Co.	3	1 0 0	1	420	3/4	80	60	4278

SHAND AND MASON--Steam ready at 150 lbs.; started at 7h. 3m. 32s.; stopped at 7h. 12m. 5s. to put on an additional length of hose; worked well throughout.

MERRYWEATHER AND SON--Steam ready at 110 lbs.; commenced work at 3h. 43m. 30s.; pumps primed.

LEE AND CO.--Steam ready, started at 2h. 1m. 0s.; worked well, without any stoppage.

AWARDS.

At a meeting of the Committee held on the 8th July, 1863, his Grace the Duke of Sutherland in the Chair, the following prizes were awarded:--

LARGE CLASS.

Messrs. Merryweather & Sons, 1st Prize, 250l. Messrs. Shand & Mason 2nd Prize, 100l. Mr. W. Roberts, highly commended.

SMALL CLASS.

Messrs. Shand & Mason 1st Prize, 250l. Messrs. W. Lee & Co. 2nd Prize, 100l.

(Signed) On behalf of the Committee,

SUTHERLAND, CHAIRMAN. E. M. SHAW, HON. SEC.

From the above trials it was found that the first prize large-class engine weighed 6504 lbs., and delivered in one hour 11,366 gallons, being at the rate of 196 gallons for each hundred-weight of the engine; while the first prize small-class engine delivered in the same time 8142 gallons, or 276 for each hundred-weight of the engine, showing that the latter engine delivered nearly one-half more water in proportion to its weight, than was delivered by the large one, the conditions of the two trials being the same.

As the greatest amount of power in the smallest possible bulk and weight, was considered most available for use at London fires, the Committee of the London Fire Brigade, although not in a position, for the reasons already stated, to purchase additional steam fire-engines, commenced hiring Shand, Mason, and Co.'s prize engines, and at the close of 1865 had four such in use in this manner.

The Metropolitan Fire Brigade, an extension of the late London Fire Brigade, has now (May, 1866) the following steam fire-engines in use:--The Floating Steam Fire-engine, by Shand and Mason, in 1855; a Land Steam Fire-engine by Easton and Amos, which was worked at the Crystal Palace trials, and is now used in a barge as a floating engine; one by Roberts, which was also worked at the Crystal Palace; three by Merryweather and Sons; and fifteen of Shand, Mason, and Co.'s Land Steam Fire-engines.

METROPOLITAN FIRE BRIGADE.

The disastrous results of the great fire at Tooley-street, in 1861, at which Mr. Braidwood lost his life, fully demonstrated the inadequacy (in men and appliances) of the fire brigade supported by the insurance offices, and as these bodies declined extending their establishment so as to meet the wants of the whole of the metropolis, a Parliamentary inquiry was instituted, which resulted in the passing of the following Act:--

ANNO VICESIMO OCTAVO & VICESIMO NONO

VICTORI?REGIN?

CAP. XC.

An Act for the Establishment of a Fire Brigade within the Metropolis. [5th July, 1865.]

WHEREAS it is expedient to make further provision for the protection of life and property from fire within the metropolis: Be it enacted by the Queen's most Excellent Majesty, by and with the advice and consent of the Lords Spiritual and Temporal, and Commons, in this present Parliament assembled, and by the authority of the same, as follows:

Preliminary.

1. This Act may be cited for all purposes as the "Metropolitan Fire Brigade Act, 1865."

2. For the purposes of this Act the "Metropolis" shall mean the City of London and all other parishes and places for the time being within the jurisdiction of the Metropolitan Board of Works:

"Insurance Company" shall include any persons corporate or unincorporate, or any person carrying on the business of fire insurance.

3. The expression "Metropolis Local Management Acts" shall mean the Acts following; that is to say, "The Metropolis Management Act, 1855," "The Metropolis Management Amendment Act, 1856," and "The Metropolis Management Amendment Act, 1862."

Establishment and Duties of Fire Brigade.

4. On and after the first day of January one thousand eight hundred and

sixty-six the duty of extinguishing fires and protecting life and property in case of fire shall within the metropolis be deemed for the purposes of this Act to be entrusted to the Metropolitan Board of Works; and with a view to the performance of that duty it shall be lawful for them to provide and maintain an efficient force of firemen, and to furnish them with all such fire engines, horses, accoutrements, tools, and implements as may be necessary for the complete equipment of the force, or conducive to the efficient performance of their duties.

5. The said Board, hereinafter referred to as the Board, may take on lease, purchase, or otherwise acquire stations for engines, stables, houses for firemen, and such other houses, buildings, or land as they may think requisite for carrying into effect the purposes of this Act, and may from time to time sell any property acquired by or vested in them for the purposes of this Act:

The Board may also contract with any company or persons authorized to establish the same for the establishment of telegraphic communication between the several stations in which their fire engines or firemen are placed, and between any of such stations and other parts of the metropolis.

6. On and after the said first day of January one thousand eight hundred and sixty-six, all stations, fire-engines, fire escapes, plant, and other property belonging to or used by the fire engine establishment of the insurance companies in the metropolis shall vest in or be conveyed or assigned to the Board for all the estate and interest of the said companies therein, upon trust to be applied by the Board to the purposes of this Act, but subject to all legal liabilities and obligations attaching thereto, including the payment of all pensions that have been granted to the members of the said Fire Engine Establishment, according to a list that has been furnished to the chairman of the said Board by the chief officer of the said fire-engine establishment, and all trustees for the same shall be indemnified against such liabilities and obligations. The Board may also, if they think fit, purchase the stations, fire-engines, and plant belonging to any parish, place, or body of persons within their jurisdiction.

7. The force of firemen established under this Act, hereinafter called the Metropolitan Fire Brigade, shall be under the command of an officer, to be called the chief officer of the Metropolitan Fire Brigade.

The chief officer and men composing the said fire brigade shall be appointed and removed at the pleasure of the Board.

8. The Board shall pay such salaries as they think expedient to the said fire brigade. They may also make such regulations as they think fit with respect to the compensation to be made to them in case of accident, or to their wives or families in case of their death; also with respect to the pensions or allowances to be paid to them in case of retirement; also with respect to the gratuities to be paid to persons giving notices of fires; also with respect to gratuities by way of a gross sum or annual payment to be from time to time awarded to any member of the said force, or to any other person, for extraordinary services performed in cases of fire; also with respect to gratuities to turncocks belonging to waterworks from which a supply of water is quickly derived.

9. The Board may by byelaws make regulations for the training, discipline, and good conduct of the men belonging to the said fire brigade, for their speedy attendance with engines, fire escapes, and all necessary implements on the occasion of any alarm of fire, and generally for the maintenance in a due state of efficiency of the said brigade, and may annex to any breach of such regulations penalties not exceeding in amount forty shillings, but no byelaw under this section shall be of any validity unless it is made and confirmed in manner directed by the Metropolis Local Management Acts; and all the provisions of the said Acts relating to byelaws shall, with the necessary variations, apply to any byelaws made in pursuance of this Act.

10. The vestry of any parish or place in the metropolis may allow such compensation as they think just to any engine keeper or other person employed in the service of fire engines who has hitherto been paid out of any rate raiseable in such parish or place, and who is deprived of his employment by or in consequence of the passing of this Act, and any compensation so allowed shall be paid out of the rate out of which the salary of the officer so compensated was payable.

11. The Board may make such arrangements as they think fit as to establishing fire escapes throughout the metropolis. They may for that purpose contribute to the funds of the Royal Society for the Protection of Life

from Fire, or of any existing society that provides fire escapes, or may purchase or take by agreement the property of any existing society in their stations and fire escapes, and generally may maintain such fire escapes and do such things as they think expedient towards aiding persons to escape from fire; and any expenses incurred by them in pursuance of this section shall be deemed to be expenses incurred in carrying into effect this Act.

12. On the occasion of a fire, the chief or other officer in charge of the fire brigade may, in his discretion, take the command of any volunteer fire brigade or other persons who voluntarily place their services at his disposal, and may remove, or order any fireman to remove, any persons who interfere by their presence with the operations of the fire brigade, and generally he may take any measures that appear expedient for the protection of life and property, with power by himself or his men to break into or through, or take possession of, or pull down any premises for the purpose of putting an end to a fire, doing as little damage as possible; he may also on any such occasion cause the water to be shut off from the mains and pipes of any district, in order to give a greater supply and pressure of water in the district in which the fire has occurred; and no water company shall be liable to any penalty or claim by reason of any interruption of the supply of water occasioned only by compliance with the provisions of this section.

All police constables shall be authorized to aid the fire brigade in the execution of their duties. They may close any street in or near which a fire is burning, and they may of their own motion, or on the request of the chief or other officer of the fire brigade, remove any persons who interfere by their presence with the operations of the fire brigade.

Any damage occasioned by the fire brigade in the due execution of their duties shall be deemed to be damage by fire within the meaning of any policy of insurance against fire.

Expenses.

13. Every insurance company that insures from fire any property in the metropolis shall pay annually to the Metropolitan Board of Works, by way of contribution toward the expenses of carrying this Act into effect, a sum after the rate of thirty-five pounds in the one million pounds on the gross amounts

insured by it, except by way of reassurance, in respect of property in the metropolis for a year, and at a like rate for any fractional part of a million, and for any fractional part of a year as well as for any number of years for which the insurance may be made, renewed, or continued.

The said payments by insurance companies shall be made quarterly in advance, on the 1st of January, 1st of April, 1st of July, and 1st of October in every year; the first of such payments to be made on the 1st of January one thousand eight hundred and sixty-six, and such first payment and the other payments for the year one thousand eight hundred and sixty-six to be based upon the amounts insured by the several companies in respect of property in the metropolis in the year ending the twenty-fourth of December one thousand eight hundred and sixty-four: provided that any insurance company which at the time of the passing of this Act contributes to the expenses of the said fire engine establishment may, in respect of all payments to be made by it in the years one thousand eight hundred and sixty-six and one thousand eight hundred and sixty-seven, but not afterwards, contribute after the yearly rate of thirty-five pounds in one million pounds of the business in respect of which it contributes to the said fire engine establishment for the present year, according to a return which has been furnished to the chairman of the said Metropolitan Board, instead of in the manner in this Act provided.

14. All contributions due from an insurance company to the Board in pursuance of this Act shall be deemed to be specialty debts due from the company to the Board, and be recovered accordingly.

15. For the purpose of ascertaining the amount to be contributed by every such insurance company as aforesaid, every insurance company insuring property from fire in the metropolis shall, on the thirtieth day of December one thousand eight hundred and sixty-five, with respect to the amounts insured in the year one thousand eight hundred and sixty-four, and on the 1st of June one thousand eight hundred and sixty-six, and on every succeeding 1st of June, or on such other days as the Metropolitan Board of Works may appoint, make a return to the said Board, in such form as they may require, of the gross amount insured by it in respect of property in the metropolis.

There shall be annexed to the return so made a declaration made by the secretary or other officer performing the duties of secretary of the company by whom it is made, stating that he has examined the return with the books of the company, and that to the best of his knowledge, information, and belief, it contains a true and faithful account of the gross amount of the sums insured by the company to which he belongs in respect of property in the metropolis.

The return made in the June of one year shall not come into effect till the 1st of January of the succeeding year, and shall be the basis of the contributions for that year.

16. If any insurance company makes default in making such returns to the Board as are required by this Act, it shall be liable to a penalty not exceeding five pounds for every day during which it is so in default.

17. The secretary or other officer having the custody of the books and papers of any insurance company that is required to pay a contribution to the Board in pursuance of this Act shall allow any officer appointed by the Board to inspect, during the hours of business, any books and papers that will enable him to ascertain the amount of property insured by such company in the metropolis, and the amount for which it is insured, and to make extracts from such books or papers; and any secretary or other such officer as aforesaid of a company failing to comply with the requisitions of this section in respect of such inspections and extracts shall be liable on summary conviction to a penalty not exceeding five pounds for each offence.

18. The Commissioners of Her Majesty's Treasury shall pay or cause to be paid to the Board by way of contribution to the expenses of maintaining the fire brigade such sums as Parliament may from time to time grant for that purpose, not exceeding in any one year the sum of ten thousand pounds.

19. For the purpose of defraying all expenses that may be incurred by the Board in carrying into effect this Act which are not otherwise provided for, the Board may from time to time issue their precepts to the overseers of the poor of every parish or place within the metropolis, requiring the overseers to pay over the amount mentioned in the precepts to the Treasurer of the Board, or into a bank to be named in the precepts, within forty days from the delivery of the precept.

The overseers shall comply with the requisitions of any such precept by paying the sums mentioned out of any monies in their hands applicable to the relief of the poor, or by levying the amount required as part of the rate for the relief of the poor, but no contribution required to be paid by any parish or place under this section shall exceed in the whole in any one year the rate of one halfpenny in the pound on the full and fair annual value of property rateable to the relief of the poor within the said parish or place, such full and fair annual value to be computed in all parts of the metropolis, exclusive of the city of London, according to the last valuation for the time being acted on in assessing the county rate, or, where there is no county rate, according to a like estimate or basis; and no liberty, precinct, or place, shall be exempt from the rate leviable for the purposes of this Act by reason of its being extra-parochial or otherwise; and in default of proper officers in any liberty, precinct, or place, to assess or levy the said rate, the Board may appoint such officers, and add the amount of any expenses so incurred to the amount to be raised by the next succeeding rate in such liberty, precinct, or place.

Overseers shall, for the purposes of levying any amount required to be levied by them under this Act, have the same powers and be subject to the same obligations as in levying a rate for the relief of the poor.

The word "Overseers" shall include any persons or bodies of persons authorized or required to make and collect or cause to be collected rates applicable to the relief of the poor; and such persons or bodies shall pay to the Board the amount so mentioned in the precept out of the said rates.

20. In case the amount ordered by any such precept as aforesaid to be paid by the overseers of any parish or place be not paid in manner directed by such precept and within the time therein specified for that purpose, it shall be lawful for any justice of the peace, upon the complaint by the Board or by any person authorized by the Board, to issue his warrant for levying the amount or so much thereof as may be in arrear by distress and sale of the goods of all or any of the said overseers, and in case the goods of all the overseers be not sufficient to pay the same, the arrears thereof shall be added to the amount of the next levy which is directed to be made in such parish or place for the purposes of this Act, and shall be collected by the like methods.

21. The Board may, with the consent of the Commissioners of Her Majesty's Treasury, borrow any sum not exceeding forty thousand pounds, and apply the same for the purposes of this Act; and all powers contained in the Metropolis Local Management Acts authorizing the Board to borrow money, or any commissioners or persons to lend money to the Board, and all other provisions as to the mode of borrowing, the repayment of principal or interest, or in anywise relating to borrowing by the Board, shall be deemed to apply and to extend to this Act in the same manner as if the monies borrowed in pursuance of this Act were monies borrowed for the purpose of defraying the expenses of the Metropolis Local Management Acts, or one or more of those acts. The Board shall apply the monies received by them under this Act in liquidation of the principal and interest of the monies so borrowed, but no creditor shall be concerned to see to such application, or be liable for any misapplication of the monies received or borrowed by the Board in pursuance of this Act.

MISCELLANEOUS.

22. Where any chief officer, or other person who has been employed by the Board in any capacity under this Act, and has been discharged therefrom, continues to occupy any house or building that may be provided for his use, or any part thereof, after one week's notice in writing from the Board to deliver up possession thereof, it shall be lawful for any police magistrate, on the oath of one witness, stating such notice to have been given, by warrant under his hand to order any constable to enter into the house or building occupied by such discharged chief officer or other person as aforesaid, and to remove him and his family and servants therefrom, and afterwards to deliver the possession thereof to the Board, as effectually, to all intents and purposes, as the sheriff having jurisdiction within the place where such house or building is situate might lawfully do by virtue of a writ of possession or a judgment at law.

23. If the chimney of any house or other building within the metropolis is on fire, the occupier of such house or building shall be liable to a penalty not exceeding twenty shillings; but if such occupier proves that he has incurred such penalty by reason of the neglect or wilful default of any other person, he may recover summarily from such person the whole or any part of the

penalty he may have incurred as occupier.

24. All penalties imposed by this Act, or by any byelaw made in pursuance thereof, and all expenses and other sums due to the Board in pursuance of this Act, in respect of which no mode of recovery is prescribed, may be recovered summarily before two justices in manner directed by the Act of the session holden in the eleventh and twelfth years of the reign of her present Majesty, chapter forty-three, or any Act amending the same, and when so recovered shall be paid to the treasurer of the Board, notwithstanding any police act or other act of parliament directing a different appropriation of such monies.

25. Any dispute or other matter which is by this Act directed to be determined summarily by two justices shall be deemed to be a matter in respect of which a complaint is made upon which they have authority by law to make an order for payment of money within the meaning of the said Act of the session holden in the eleventh and twelfth years of the reign of her present Majesty, chapter forty-three, or any Act amending the same.

26. Any act, power, or jurisdiction hereby authorized to be done or exercised by two justices may be done or exercised by the following magistrates within their respective jurisdictions; that is to say, by any metropolitan police magistrate sitting alone at a police court or other appointed place, or by the Lord Mayor of the City of London, or any alderman of the said City, sitting alone or with others at the Mansion House or Guildhall.

27. The accounts of the Board in respect of expenses incurred by them under this Act shall be audited in the same manner as if they were expenses incurred under the said Metropolis Local Management Acts, and the Board shall in each year make a report to one of her Majesty's principal Secretaries of State of all acts done and expenditure incurred by them in pursuance of this Act, and that report shall be laid before Parliament within one month after the commencement of the session.

28. The Board may delegate any powers conferred on them by this Act to a committee of their body; and such committee shall, to the extent to which such powers are delegated, be deemed to be the Board within the meaning of this Act.

29. If the companies insuring property within the metropolis, or any such number of them as may in the opinion of the said Board be sufficient, establish a force of men charged with the duty of attending at fires and saving insured property, it shall be the duty of the Fire Brigade, with the sanction of the Board, and subject to any regulations that may be made by the Board, to afford the necessary assistance to that force in the performance of their duties, and, upon the application of any officer of that force, to hand over to their custody property that may be saved from fire; and no charge shall be made by the said Board for the services thus rendered by the fire brigade.

30. It shall be lawful for the Board, when occasion requires, to permit any part of the fire brigade establishment, with their engines, escapes, and other implements, to proceed beyond the limits of the metropolis for the purpose of extinguishing fires. In such case the owner and occupier of the property where the fire has occurred shall be jointly and severally liable to defray all the expenses that may be incurred by the Fire Brigade in attending the fire, and shall pay to the Board a reasonable charge for the attendance of the Fire Brigade, and the use of their engines, escapes, and other implements. In case of difference between the Board and the owner and occupier of such property, or either of them, the amount of the expenses, as well as the propriety of the Fire Brigade attending such fire (if the propriety thereof be disputed), shall be summarily determined by two justices. In default of payment, any expenses under this section may be recovered by the Board in a summary manner.

The Board may also permit any part of the Fire Brigade Establishment to be employed on special services upon such terms of remuneration as the said Board may think just.

31. The Metropolitan Fire Brigade shall in the morning of each day, with the exception of Sundays, send information, by post or otherwise, to all the insurance offices contributing for the purposes of this Act, of all fires which have taken place within the metropolis since the preceding return, in such form as may be agreed upon between the Board and the said companies.

32. All the powers now exercised by any local body or officer within the

metropolis as respects fireplugs shall henceforth be exercised by the Board, and the Board shall be entitled to receive copies or extracts of all plans kept by any water company under the provision of the Act of the session of the fifteenth and sixteenth years of her Majesty, chapter eighty-four; and every such water company shall provide at the expense of the Board in any mains or pipes within the metropolis plugs for the supply of water in case of fire at such places, of such dimensions, and in such form as the Board may require, and the Fire Brigade shall be at liberty to make such use thereof as they may deem necessary for the purpose of extinguishing any fire; and every such company shall deposit keys of all their fireplugs at such places as may be appointed by the Board, and the Board may put up on any house or building a public notice in some conspicuous place in each street in which a fireplug is situated, showing its situation.

33. "Owner" in this Act shall mean the person for the time being receiving the rackrent of the premises in connexion with which the word is used, either on his own account or as agent or trustee for some other person, or who would receive the same if the premises were let at rackrent.

Repeal.

34. On and after the first day of January, one thousand eight hundred and sixty-six, there shall be repealed so much as is unrepealed of an Act passed in the fourteenth year of his late Majesty King George the Third, chapter seventy-eight, and intituled an Act for the further and better regulation of buildings and party walls, and for the more effectually preventing mischief by fire, within the Cities of London and Westminster and the liberties thereof, and other the parishes, precincts, and places within the weekly bills of mortality, the parishes of St. Marylebone, Paddington, St. Pancras, and St. Luke, at Chelsea, in the County of Middlesex, and for indemnifying, under certain conditions, builders and other persons against the penalties to which they are or may be liable for erecting buildings within the limits aforesaid contrary to law, with the exception of sections eighty-three and eighty-six which shall remain in full force, but such repeal shall not affect any penalty or liability incurred under the repealed sections.

35. On and after the first day of January, one thousand eight hundred and sixty-six, section forty-four of an Act passed in the session holden in the third

and fourth years of the reign of King William the Fourth, chapter ninety, shall be repealed so far as respects any parish or place within the limits of the metropolis as defined by this Act; provided that the repeal of the said section shall not affect the power of the churchwardens and overseers of any parish or place to contribute to the funds of any society that at the time of the passing of this Act maintains fire escapes in such parish or place, unless and until the Board purchase the property of such society, or otherwise provide fire escapes in such parish or place.

* * * * *

In accordance with the provisions of the above recited Act of Parliament, the London Fire Brigade of the Insurance Offices is now being extended to meet the requirements of the whole of London, under the title of the Metropolitan Fire Brigade, with Captain E. M. Shaw, Mr. Braidwood's successor, as chief officer.

* * * * *

www.ingramcontent.com/pod-product-compliance
Lightning Source LLC
Chambersburg PA
CBHW062008280526
45787CB00005B/2021